FROM
UNION SQUARE
TO ROME

FROM UNION SQUARE TO ROME

DOROTHY DAY

ORBIS BOOKS

Maryknoll, New York 10545

Founded in 1970, Orbis Books endeavors to publish works that enlighten the mind, nourish the spirit, and challenge the conscience. The publishing arm of the Maryknoll Fathers and Brothers, Orbis seeks to explore the global dimensions of the Christian faith and mission, to invite dialogue with diverse cultures and religious traditions, and to serve the cause of reconciliation and peace. The books published reflect the views of their authors and do not represent the official position of the Maryknoll Society. To learn more about Maryknoll and Orbis Books, please visit our website at www.maryknoll.org.

Library of Congress Cataloging-in-Publication Data
Day, Dorothy, 1897-1980.
    From Union Square to Rome / Dorothy Day.
      p. cm.
    Originally published: Silver Spring, Md. : Preservation of the Faith Press, 1938.
    ISBN-13: 978-1-57075-667-2 (pbk.)
    1. Day, Dorothy, 1897-1980. 2. Catholic converts – United States – Biography. I. Title.
BX4668.D3A32 2006
248.2′46092 – dc22

                         2006009455

TO MY BROTHER

CONTENTS

FOREWORD

D OROTHY DAY'S first memoir of her conversion, *From Union Square to Rome*, was published in 1938 by Preservation of the Faith Press. It attracted little attention, and was eventually overshadowed by the publication in 1952 of her classic autobiography, *The Long Loneliness*. There she included this brief reference to her earlier work: "When I wrote the story of my conversion twelve years ago, I left out all my sins but told of all the things which had brought me to God, all the beautiful things, all the remembrances of God that had haunted me, pursued me over the years, so that when my daughter was born, in grateful joy I turned to God and became a Catholic."

Read in the light of her more famous memoir, it is fair to regard *From Union Square to Rome* as something of a first draft. Both books cover similar ground: Day's early life, her involvement in the radical movements of her day, and the succession of events, both sad and joyous, that brought about her conversion to Catholicism.

The earlier book does not, in fact, leave out all her sins. But there is a more striking omission: the decision to conclude her narrative before her fateful meeting with Peter

Maurin and the launching of the Catholic Worker movement, a story that occupies the final third of *The Long Loneliness*. In writing *From Union Square to Rome*, she had a more specific purpose. Addressing her former comrades on the Left — in the person of her brother — she sought to account for her embrace of the Catholic faith, a move they regarded as a betrayal of the radical cause.

Many factors played a role in this conversion, including the example of certain Catholics she met along the way. Even as a child she perceived that they had something she lacked — a sense of balance and order, some access to the transcendent. All her life, Day writes, she was "haunted by God" and the sense that there was a deeper, spiritual dimension to life. She experienced this in moments of dejection, such as her lonely stints in jail, as well as moments of joy, such as the birth of her daughter. It was this latter experience, recorded here in her journals of the time, that finally prompted her leap of faith. She had found the pearl of great price for which she was prepared to sacrifice everything.

But among all those many "things that had brought her to God," Day gives special credit to her experiences in the radical movement. For years she traveled among an eclectic circle of socialists, anarchists, literary bohemians, and assorted rebels, unified mainly by their opposition to the status quo and their longing for a better world. In becoming a Catholic, Day was determined not to turn her back on all that was good and noble in these principles: the spirit of solidarity, reverence for the poor and oppressed, respect for the dignity of work, the willingness to suffer for a cause, the spirit of idealism, and the capacity for indignation. In the Gospels, all this found a wider reference.

In one of her more memorable declarations, she states: "Let it be said that I found [God] through His poor, and in a moment of joy I turned to Him. I have said, sometimes flippantly, that the mass of bourgeois smug Christians who denied Christ in His poor made me turn to Communism, and that it was the Communists and working with them that made me turn to God."

There is some indication that Day was never entirely pleased with the title of this book. It suggested a chasm between the world of radical agitation — Union Square — and the world of faith, whereas in fact Day's life would bridge these worlds. Nothing symbolized this so clearly as the decision to launch *The Catholic Worker* on May 1, 1933, at a Communist rally in Union Square.

But Day chose to save that story for another book.

Simone Weil wrote an essay on what she called "the implicit forms of the love of God," including friendship, love of neighbor, the beauty of the world, and religious practice. All these, she wrote, bear the grace of God and the capacity to elevate the soul, even where God is not explicitly acknowledged. All these "implicit" forms are present in Day's story. But in *From Union Square to Rome* she adds another: devotion to the poor and a passion for justice. Quoting the novelist François Mauriac, she writes: "It is impossible for any one of those who has real charity in his heart not to serve Christ. Even some of those who think they hate Him, have consecrated their lives to Him; for Jesus is disguised and masked in the midst of men, hidden among the poor, among the sick, among prisoners, among strangers."

In this book, Day describes the steps by which such implicit love of God became explicit, and how she came to accept the faith that was "always in [her] heart." And yet, in every conversion there is an element of mystery, a factor that cannot be reasoned or put into words. How many of her "brothers" were persuaded by this apologetic exercise is impossible to say. The mystery lies beyond words, as Day hinted in this curious pronouncement — the closest she ever came to a Zen riddle: "This exaltation of the articulate obscures the fact that there are millions of people in this world who feel and in some way carry on courageously even though they cannot talk or reason brilliantly. This very talk may obscure everything that we know nothing of now, and who knows but that silence may lead us to it."

Robert Ellsberg

INTRODUCTION

T HIS IS NOT an autobiography. Neither is it the complete story of the author's life. The clock has been turned back twenty years or more while the author writes of those incidents and people who helped her along the path to God. There is nothing in this book concerning the movement in which she finds herself embroiled today. In fact these few pages stop at the threshold of that movement which is known and talked about in many places on this earth. There is nothing herein of controversy though no doubt many passages will provoke criticism. It is a human document which cost much effort to write. Why then does she write it?

Many of her relatives and friends, who are Communists, keep asking with dismay: "How could you become a Catholic?" After all, she did believe with them that "religion is the opium of the people." The circumstances that led to her conversion are strange — so strange that even now after many years in the Church there are those who do not believe that she is a Catholic, but rather an enemy boring from within.

This story she addresses to all those people, in the person of her brother. Some of the chapters have already appeared in *The Preservation of the Faith* magazine, and in response to the requests of many readers it appears in book form. Parts of it have appeared in *America* and *The Sign* and to these publications we are grateful for the permission to reprint.

Much more could be written by way of introduction, but it seems best to leave this as it is. This point, however, must be borne in mind when reading this book: It is addressed to her brother, to a Communist. It is "dipping back into the past" to the time when she herself believed what many Communists profess to believe today. She cannot always explain herself; it is not always pleasant. As has been said, the narrative ends with her conversion, when her real work began. Whether you are in agreement with that work or not, you are sure to be impressed with the struggle toward God that immediately preceded it.

Chapter One

WHY

I T IS DIFFICULT for me to dip back into the past, yet it is a job that must be done, and it hangs over my head like a cloud. St. Peter said that we must give a reason for the faith that is in us, and I am trying to give you those reasons.

This is not an autobiography. I am a woman forty years old and I am not trying to set down the story of my life. Please keep that in mind as you read. While it is true that often horror for one's sins turns one to God, what I want to bring out in this book is a succession of events that led me to His feet, glimpses of Him that I received through many years which made me feel the vital need of Him and of religion. I will try to trace for you the steps by which I came to accept the faith that I believe was always in my heart. For this reason, most of the time I will speak of the good I encountered even amid surroundings and people who tried to reject God.

The mark of the atheist is the deliberate rejection of God. And since you do not reject God or deliberately embrace evil, then you are not an atheist. Because you doubt and deny in words what your heart and mind do not deny, you consider yourself an agnostic.

Though I felt the strong, irresistible attraction to good, yet there was also, at times, a deliberate choosing of evil. How far I was led to choose it, it is hard to say. How far professors, companions, and reading influenced my way of life does not matter now. The fact remains that there was much of deliberate choice in it. Most of the time it was "following the devices and desires of my own heart." Sometimes it was perhaps the Baudelairean idea of choosing "the downward path which leads to salvation." Sometimes it was of choice, of free will, though perhaps at the time I would have denied free will. And so, since it was deliberate, with recognition of its seriousness, it was grievous mortal sin and may the Lord forgive me. It was the arrogance and suffering of youth. It was pathetic, little, and mean in its very excuse for itself.

Was this desire to be with the poor and the mean and abandoned not unmixed with a distorted desire to be with the dissipated? Mauriac tells of this subtle pride and hypocrisy: "There is a kind of hypocrisy which is worse than that of the Pharisees; it is to hide behind Christ's example in order to follow one's own lustful desires and to seek out the company of the dissolute."

I write these things now because sometimes when I am writing I am seized with fright at my presumption. I am afraid, too, of not telling the truth or of distorting the truth. I cannot guarantee that I do not for I am writing

4

of the past. But my whole perspective has changed and when I look for causes of my conversion, sometimes it is one thing and sometimes it is another that stands out in my mind.

Much as we want to know ourselves, we do not really know ourselves. Do we really want to see ourselves as God sees us, or even as our fellow human beings see us? Could we bear it, weak as we are? You know that feeling of contentment in which we sometimes go about, clothed in it, as it were, like a garment, content with the world and with ourselves. We are ourselves and we would be no one else. We are glad that God made us as we are and we would not have had Him make us like anyone else. According to the weather, our state of health, we have moods of purely animal happiness and content. We do not want to be given that clear inward vision which discloses to us our most secret faults. In the Psalms there is that prayer, "Deliver me from my secret sins." We do not really know how much pride and self-love we have until someone whom we respect or love suddenly turns against us. Then some sudden affront, some sudden offense we take, reveals to us in all its glaring distinctness our self-love, and we are ashamed. . . .

I write in the very beginning of finding the Bible and the impression it made on me. I must have read it a good deal, for many passages remained with me through my earlier years to return and haunt me. Do you know the Psalms? They were what I read most when I was in jail in Occoquan. I read with a sense of coming back to something that

I had lost. There was an echoing in my heart. And how can anyone who has known human sorrow and human joy fail to respond to these words?

"Out of the depths I have cried to thee, O Lord:
Lord, hear my voice. Let thy ears be attentive to the voice of my supplication.
If thou, O Lord, wilt mark iniquities:
Lord, who shall stand it.
For with thee there is merciful forgiveness: and by reason of thy law, I have waited for thee,
O Lord. My soul hath relied on his word: my soul hath hoped in the Lord.
From the morning watch even until night, let Israel hope in the Lord.
Because with the Lord there is mercy; and with him plentiful redemption.
And he shall redeem Israel from all his iniquities."

"Hear, O Lord, my prayer: give ear to my supplication in thy truth:
hear me in thy justice.
And enter not into judgment with thy servant: for in thy sight no man living shall be justified.
For the enemy hath persecuted my soul: he hath brought down my life to the earth.
He hath made me to dwell in darkness as those that have been dead of old:

And my spirit is in anguish within me: my heart
within me is troubled.

I remembered the days of old, I meditated on all thy
works:

I meditated upon the works of thy hands.

I stretched forth my hands to thee: my soul is as
earth without water unto thee.

Hear me speedily O Lord; my spirit hath fainted
away.

Turn not away thy face from me, lest I be like unto
them that go down into the pit.

Cause me to hear thy mercy in the morning; for in
thee have I hoped.

Make the way known to me, wherein I should walk:
for I have lifted up my soul to thee."

All through those weary first days in jail when I was in
solitary confinement, the only thoughts that brought comfort to my soul were those lines in the Psalms that expressed
the terror and misery of man suddenly stricken and abandoned. Solitude and hunger and weariness of spirit — these
sharpened my perceptions so that I suffered not only my
own sorrow but the sorrows of those about me. I was no
longer myself. I was man. I was no longer a young girl, part
of a radical movement seeking justice for those oppressed,
I was the oppressed. I was that drug addict, screaming and
tossing in her cell, beating her head against the wall. I was
that shoplifter who for rebellion was sentenced to solitary.

I was that woman who had killed her children, who had murdered her lover.

The blackness of hell was all about me. The sorrows of the world encompassed me. I was like one gone down into the pit. Hope had forsaken me. I was that mother whose child had been raped and slain. I was the mother who had borne the monster who had done it. I was even that monster, feeling in my own heart every abomination.

As I read this over, it seems, indeed, over-emotional and an exaggerated statement of the reactions of a young woman in jail. But if you live for long in the slums of cities, if you are in constant contact with sins and suffering, it is indeed rarely that so overwhelming a realization comes upon one. It often has seemed to me that most people instinctively protect themselves from being touched too closely by the suffering of others. They turn from it, and they make this a habit. The tabloids with their presentation of crime testify to the repulsive truth that there is a secret excitement and pleasure in reading of the sufferings of others. One might say there is a surface sensation in the realization of the tragedy in the lives of others. But one who has accepted hardship and poverty as the way in life in which to walk, lays himself open to this susceptibility to the sufferings of others.

And yet if it were not the Holy Spirit that comforted me, how could I have been comforted, how could I have endured, how could I have lived in hope?

The Imitation of Christ is a book that followed me through my days. Again and again I came across copies of it and the reading of it brought me comfort. I felt in the background of my life a waiting force that would lift me up eventually.

I later became acquainted with the poem of Francis Thompson, *The Hound of Heaven,* and was moved by its power. Eugene O'Neill recited it first to me in the back room of a saloon on Sixth Avenue where the Province-town players and playwrights used to gather after the performances.

"I fled Him, down the nights and down the days;
I fled Him, down the arches of the years;
I fled Him, down the labyrinthine ways
Of my own mind; and in the mist of tears
I hid from Him."

Through all my daily life, in those I came in contact with, in the things I read and heard, I felt that sense of being followed, of being desired; a sense of hope and expectation.

Through those years I read all of Dostoevsky's novels and it was, as Berdyaev says, a profound spiritual experience. The scene in *Crime and Punishment* where the young prostitute reads from the New Testament to Raskolnikov, sensing the sin more profound than her own, which weighed upon him; that story, *The Honest Thief;* those passages in *The Brothers Karamazov;* the sayings of Father

Zossima, Mitya's conversion in jail, the very legend of the Grand Inquisitor, all this helped to lead me on. The characters, Alyosha and *The Idiot,* testified to Christ in us. I was moved to the depths of my being by the reading of these books during my early twenties when I, too, was tasting the bitterness and the dregs of life and shuddered at its harshness and cruelty.

Do you remember that little story that Grushenka told in *The Brothers Karamazov?* "Once upon a time there was a peasant woman and a very wicked woman she was. And she died and did not leave a single good deed behind. The devils caught her and plunged her into a lake of fire. So her guardian angel stood and wondered what good deed of hers he could remember to tell God. 'She once pulled up an onion in her garden,' said he, 'and gave it to a beggar woman.' And God answered: 'You take that onion then, hold it out to her in the lake, and let her take hold and be pulled out. And if you pull her out of the lake, let her come to Paradise, but if the onion breaks, then the woman must stay where she is.' The angel ran to the woman and held out the onion to her. 'Come,' said he, 'catch hold, and I'll pull you out.' And he began cautiously pulling her out. He had just pulled her out, when the other sinners in the lake, seeing how she was being drawn out, began catching hold of her so as to be pulled out with her. But she was a very wicked woman and she began kicking them. 'I'm to be pulled out, not you. It's my onion, not yours.' As soon as she said that, the onion broke. And the woman fell into the lake and she is burning there to this day. So the angel wept and went away."

Sometimes in thinking and wondering at God's goodness to me, I have thought that it was because I gave away an onion. Because I sincerely loved His poor, He taught me to know Him. And when I think of the little I ever did, I am filled with hope and love for all those others devoted to the cause of social justice.

"What glorious hope!" Mauriac writes. "There are all those who will discover that their neighbor is Jesus himself, although they belong to the mass of those who do not know Christ or who have forgotten Him. And nevertheless they will find themselves well loved. It is impossible for any one of those who has real charity in his heart not to serve Christ. Even some of those who think they hate Him, have consecrated their lives to Him; for Jesus is disguised and masked in the midst of men, hidden among the poor, among the sick, among prisoners, among strangers. Many who serve Him officially have never known who He was, and many who do not even know His name, will hear on the last day the words that open to them the gates of joy. 'Those children were I, and I those working men. I wept on the hospital bed. I was that murderer in his cell whom you consoled.'"

But always the glimpses of God came most when I was alone. Objectors cannot say that it was fear of loneliness and solitude and pain that made me turn to Him. It was in those few years when I was alone and most happy that I found Him. I found Him at last through joy and thanksgiving, not through sorrow.

Yet how can I say that either? Better let it be said that I found Him through His poor, and in a moment of joy I turned to Him. I have said, sometimes flippantly, that the mass of bourgeois smug Christians who denied Christ in His poor made me turn to Communism, and that it was the Communists and working with them that made me turn to God.

Communism, says our Holy Father, can be likened to a heresy, and a heresy is a distortion of the truth. Many Christians have lost sight, to a great extent, of the communal aspect of Christianity, so the collective ideal is the result. They have failed to learn a philosophy of labor, have failed to see Christ in the worker. So in Russia, the worker, instead of Christ, has been exalted. They have the dictatorship of the proletariat maintained by one man, also a dictator. The proletariat as a class has come to be considered the Messiah, the deliverer.

A mystic may be called a man in love with God. Not one who loves God, but who is *in love with God*. And this mystical love, which is an exalted emotion, leads one to love the things of Christ. His footsteps are sacred. The steps of His passion and death are retraced down through the ages. Almost every time you step into a Church you see people making the Stations of the Cross. They meditate on the mysteries of His life, death, and resurrection, and by this they are retracing with love those early scenes and identifying themselves with the actors in those scenes.

When we suffer, we are told we suffer with Christ. We are "completing the sufferings of Christ." We suffer His loneliness and fear in the garden when His friends slept. We are bowed down with Him under the weight of not only our own sins but the sins of each other, of the whole world. We are those who are sinned against and those who are sinning. We are identified with Him, one with Him. We are members of His Mystical Body.

Often there is a mystical element in the love of a radical worker for his brother, for his fellow worker. It extends to the scene of his sufferings, and those spots where he has suffered and died are hallowed. The names of places like Everett, Ludlow, Bisbee, South Chicago, Imperial Valley, Elaine, Arkansas, and all those other places where workers have suffered and died for their cause have become sacred to the worker. You know this feeling as does every other radical in the country. Through ignorance, perhaps, you do not acknowledge Christ's name, yet, I believe you are trying to love Christ in His poor, in His persecuted ones. Whenever men have laid down their lives for their fellows, they are doing it in a measure for Him. This I still firmly believe, even though you and others may not realize it.

"Inasmuch as ye have done it unto one of the least of these brethren, you have done it unto me." Feeling this as strongly as I did, is it any wonder that I was led finally to the feet of Christ?

I do not mean at all that I went around in a state of exaltation or that any radical does. Love is a matter of the will. You know yourself how during a long strike the spirit falters, how hard it is for the leaders to keep up the morale of the men and to keep the fire of hope burning within them. They have a hard time sustaining this hope themselves. Saint Teresa says that there are three attributes of the soul: memory, understanding, and will. These very leaders by their understanding of the struggle, how victory is gained very often through defeat, how every little gain benefits the workers all over the country, how, through their memory of past struggles, they are enabled to strengthen their wills to go on. It is only by exerting these faculties of the soul that one is enabled to love one's fellow. And this strength comes from God. There can be no brotherhood without the Fatherhood of God.

Take a factory where fifty per cent of the workers are themselves content, do not care about their fellows. It is hard to inspire them with the idea of solidarity. Take those workers who despise their fellow-worker, the Negro, the Hungarian, the Italian, the Irish, where race hatreds and nationalist feelings persist. It is hard to overcome their stubborn resistance with patience and with love. That is why there is coercion, the beating of scabs and strikebreakers, the threats and the hatreds that grow up. That is why in labor struggles, unless there is a wise and patient leader, there is disunity, a rending of the Mystical Body.

14

Even the most unbelieving of labor leaders have understood the expediency of patience when I have talked to them. They realize that the use of force has lost more strikes than it has won them. They realize that when there is no violence in a strike, the employer through his armed guards and strikebreakers may try to introduce this violence. It has happened again and again in labor history.

What is hard to make the labor leader understand is that we must love even the employer, unjust though he may be, that we must try to overcome his resistance by non-violent resistance, by withdrawing labor, *i.e.*, by strikes and by boycott. These are non-violent means and most effective. We must try to educate him, to convert him. We must forgive him seventy times seven just as we forgive our fellow-worker and keep trying to bring him to a sense of solidarity.

This is the part labor does not seem to understand in this country or in any country. Class war does exist. We cannot deny it. It is there. Class lines are drawn even here in America where we have always flattered ourselves that the poor boy can become president, the messenger boy, the head of the corporation. The very fact of the necessity of national security laws, old age and unemployment insurance, acknowledges the existence of a proletariat class. The employer much too often does not pay a wage sufficient for a man to care for his family in sickness and in health. The unskilled worker, who is in the majority, does not have enough to lay some by for his old age or enough to buy a home with or to buy his share in partnership. He has been too long exploited and ground down. The line has been fixed dividing the rich and the poor, the owner and the proletariat who are the unpropertied, the dispossessed.

And how to convert an employer who has evicted all his workers because they were on strike so that men, women, and children are forced to live in tents, who has called out armed guards as Rockefeller did in Ludlow, who shot into those tents and fired them so that twenty-eight women and children were burnt to death? How to forgive such a man? How to convert him? This is the question the worker asks you in the bitterness of his soul? It is only through a Christ-like love that man can forgive.

Remember Vanzetti's last words before he died in the electric chair. "I wish to tell you I am an innocent man. I never committed any crime, but sometimes some sin. I wish to forgive some people for what they are now doing to me."

He said when he was sentenced: "If it had not been for these things, I might have lived out my life talking at street corners to scorning men. I might have died unmarked, un-known, a failure. Now we are not a failure. This is our career and our triumph. Never in our full life could we hope to do such work for tolerance, for justice, for man's understanding of man, as now we do by accident. Our words, our lives, our pains — nothing! The taking of our lives — lives of a good shoemaker and a poor fish ped-dler — all! That last moment belongs to us. That agony is our triumph." He forgave those who had imprisoned him for years, who had hounded him to his death. You have read Mauriac. He was one of those of whom Mauriac was speaking when he said, "It is impossible for any one of those who has charity in his heart not to serve Christ. Even those who think they hate Him have consecrated their lives to Him."

It was from men such as these that I became convinced, little by little, of the necessity of religion and of God in my everyday life. I know now that the Catholic Church is the church of the poor, no matter what you say about the wealth of her priests and bishops. I have mentioned in these pages the few Catholics I met before my conversion, but daily I saw people coming from Mass. Never did I set foot in a Catholic church but that I saw people there at home with Him. First Fridays, novenas, and missions brought the masses thronging in and out of the Catholic churches. They were of all nationalities, of all classes, but most of all they were the poor. The very attacks made against the Church proved her Divinity to me. Nothing but a Divine institution could have survived the betrayal of Judas, the denial of Peter, the sins of many of those who professed her Faith, who were supposed to minister to her poor.

Christ is God or He is the world's greatest liar and imposter. How can you Communists who claim to revere Him as a working class leader fail to see this? And if Christ established His Church on earth with Peter as its rock, that faulty one who denied him three times, who fled from Him when he was in trouble, then I, too, wanted a share in that tender compassionate love that is so great. Christ can forgive all sins and yearn over us no matter how far we fall.

How I ramble on! I do it partly to avoid getting on to the work of this book. It will, no doubt, be disjointed, perhaps incoherent, but I have promised to write it. It entails suffering, as I told you, to write it. I have to dig into myself to get it out. I have to inflict wounds on myself. I have, perhaps, to say things that were better left unsaid.

After all, the experiences that I have had are more or less universal. Suffering, sadness, repentance, love, we all have known these. They are easiest to bear when one remembers their universality, when we remember that we are all members or potential members of the Mystical Body of Christ.

However, one does not like to write about others, thus violating their privacy, especially others near and dear. So, in what follows I have tried to leave out as much as possible of other personalities, those of our own family, and those with whom later I associated most intimately.

A conversion is a lonely experience. We do not know what is going on in the depths of the heart and soul of another. We scarcely know ourselves.

Chapter Two

CHILDHOOD

YOU ASK ME how did it all come about, this turning toward religion, and you speak of it as though I were turning away from life when all the while it was so much a part of my life.

"All my life I have been tormented by God," a character in one of Dostoevsky's books says. And that is the way it was with me. You will notice that I quote the Russian author a good deal, but that is because we both have read him. And I quote him often because he had a profound influence on my life, on my way of thinking.

I have to go back to the beginning, to my first memories of God. It will take a long time to tell it. It might be better told on one of those long walks you and I so loved to take down through the East Side, along the river late at night, through snow and ice in winter, striking out briskly as though we had some objective, and most often our only objective was to settle some problem for ourselves. There were those fall days, too, down in the country when we went out on the pier to fish, and lay there along the bulkhead, listening to the soft lap of the waves down below in the darkness. Some such setting is needed for so long a story.

It began out in California where the family had moved from New York a year before. We were living in Berkeley in a furnished house, waiting for our furniture to come around the Horn. It was Sunday afternoon in the attic. I remember the day was very chilly, though there were roses and violets and calla lilies blooming in the garden. My sister and I had been making dolls of the calla lilies, putting rosebuds for heads at the top of the long graceful blossom. Then we made perfume, crushing flowers into a bottle with a little water in it. Even now I can remember the peculiar, delicious, pungent smell.

And then I remember we were in the attic. I was sitting behind a table, pretending I was the teacher, reading aloud from a Bible that I had found. Slowly, as I read, a new personality impressed itself on me. I was being introduced to someone and I knew almost immediately that I was discovering God.

I know that I had just really discovered Him because it excited me tremendously. It was as though life were fuller, richer, more exciting in every way. Here was someone that I had never really known about before and yet felt to be One whom I would never forget, that I would never get away from. The game might grow stale, it might assume new meanings, new aspects, but life would never again be the same. I had made a great discovery.

Of course I had heard of Him previous to this. Before we moved to California your older brothers and I had gone to school in Bath Beach, and there every morning the teacher read something from the Bible and we bowed our heads on the desk and recited the Lord's Prayer. I had forgotten that until this moment of writing. It did not impress me then, and I remember now simply raising my head after the prayer to watch my breath fade upon the varnished desk.

In the family the name of God was never mentioned. Mother and father never went to church, none of us children had been baptized, and to speak of the soul was to speak immodestly, uncovering what might better remain hidden.

I can remember so many vivid impressions of early childhood. I can remember so many pictures and sights and sounds and smells. I vividly enjoyed my early years. There was so much to do and play and enjoy and read. I can even remember intense sufferings, remorse for childish sins.

But in all the first years I remember nothing about God except that routine chapter and prayer in school which I did not feel. It was that Sunday afternoon up in the dim attic and the rich, deep feeling of having a book, which would be with me through life, that stands out in my mind now.

I had been reading books for a long time, since I was four, in fact. I can remember books I read, children's stories, and the fascinating *Arabian Nights* which I read when I was six. But this was the first Bible I had ever seen. It came with the furnished house, and I wanted even then to keep it always.

Then there is one of those gaps in memory. It must have been shortly after that we moved from Berkeley to Oakland. Our furniture had come and we were established in a bungalow near open fields and woods, where windows looked out to the hills, and forest fires perfumed the air (there always seemed to be forest fires), making a haze on the changing hills.

I had not taken the Bible with me. As a matter of fact, some years passed before I took it up again. But next door down the road there was a little girl by the name of Naomi Reed. She was just my age and her mother kept a grocery store next to her house. There were brothers and sisters but no father. Mrs. Reed was a widow (the first I had ever known).

They were Methodists and regular churchgoers, and it was not long before I started going to church and Sunday school with Naomi. There was a library attached to the Sunday school and pious books to read. But best of all, there was the hymn singing. The sound of a church full of voices raised in sad or lively but always fervent airs, delighted me. It penetrated to the marrow of my bones so that the hair stood up on my arms and the skin prickled on the back of my neck. I became a regular churchgoer.

It was almost as good to hear Mrs. Reed and her children hymn singing at night before they went to bed. I loved and admired them all. How model a family life I felt them to have — peace, unity, love. I even admired the smugness, their conviction that they were of the saved and we, the non-churchgoers, were of the damned. (Somehow or other I didn't believe that for a minute, but it was part of their atmosphere, and I accepted it with them.) What I did recognize was that they had something which we did not: a belief, a faith, and the consequent order and tranquility that went with that belief.

Then Naomi stopped playing with me because I was heard to call my elder brother a bad name (I threw things besides) in a fight over whose guinea pigs were whose. I was cast into outer darkness. I was no longer invited to church. I couldn't play with Naomi any more. I took refuge with a tough gang of kids whose homes were lined with funny papers, who ran away to Idora Park, who stayed out after dark and didn't mind their mothers; and I had a very good time indeed.

The cool delicious sense of being one of the saved could not be sustained. It was hard to hold out against the whole family. I did not want to be saved alone anyway. Perhaps it was just a game, a cloak, a garment, that people put on and off. It was too much for me to think about. I bothered my head no longer about church and faith until a year later when I met my first Catholic.

We were in California until after the earthquake which shook us eastward. We were living in Oakland at the time and though I remember some years later praying fearfully during a lightning storm, I do not remember praying during that cataclysmic disturbance, the earthquake. And I remember it plainly. I was eight years old then. It was after two in the morning when it started, and it began with a fearful roaring down in the earth. It lasted for two minutes and twenty seconds, and there was plenty of time to have died of fright, yet I do not remember fear. It must have been either that I thought I was dreaming or that I was half conscious. Pictures fell from the walls, the bed rolled from one end of the polished floor to the other. My father got my brothers out of the house and my mother was able to carry my sister — God alone knew how she did it — out of the bungalow. I think the first shock was over before they got back to me.

What I remember most plainly about the earthquake was the human warmth and kindliness of everyone afterward. For days refugees poured out of burning San Francisco and camped in Idora Park and the race track in Oakland. People came in their night clothes; there were new-born babies.

Mother had always complained before about how clannish California people were, how if you were from the East they snubbed you and were loathe to make friends. But after the earthquake everyone's heart was enlarged by Christian charity. All the hard crust of worldly reserve and prudence was shed. Each person was a little child in friendliness and warmth.

Mother and all our neighbors were busy from morning to night cooking hot meals. They gave away every extra garment they possessed. They stripped themselves to the bone in giving, forgetful of the morrow. While the crisis lasted, people loved each other. They realized their own helplessness while nature "travaileth and groaneth." It was as though they were united in Christian solidarity. It makes one think of how people could, if they would, care for each other in time of stress, unjudgingly, with pity and with love.

◆ ◆ ◆

It was in Chicago, where we moved to afterward, that I met my first Catholic. It was the first time we had been really poor. We lived in an apartment over a store, on Cottage Grove Avenue. There was no upstairs, no garden, no sense of space. The tenement stretched away down the block and there were back porches and paved courtyards with never a touch of green anywhere. I remember how hungry I became for the green fields during the long hot summer that followed. There was a vacant lot over by the lake front and I used to walk down there with my sister and stand sniffing ecstatically the hot sweet smell of wild clover and listening to the sleepy sound of the crickets. But that very desire for beauty was a painful delight for me. It sharpened my senses and made me more avid in my search for it. I found it in the lake that stretched steel gray beyond the Illinois Central tracks. I found it in that one lone field of clover.

And I found a glimpse of supernatural beauty in Mrs. Barrett, mother of Kathryn and six other little Barretts, who lived upstairs.

It was Mrs. Barrett who gave me my first impulse toward Catholicism. It was around ten o'clock in the morning that I went up to Kathryn's to call for her to come out and play. There was no one on the porch or in the kitchen. The breakfast dishes had all been washed. They were long railroad apartments, those flats, and thinking the children must be in the front room, I burst in and ran through the bedrooms.

In the front bedroom Mrs. Barrett was on her knees, saying her prayers. She turned to tell me that Kathryn and the children had all gone to the store and went on with her praying. And I felt a warm burst of love toward Mrs. Barrett that I have never forgotten, a feeling of gratitude and happiness that still warms my heart when I remember her. She had God, and there was beauty and joy in her life.

All through my life what she was doing remained with me. And though I became oppressed with the problem of poverty and injustice, though I groaned at the hideous sordidness of man's lot, though there were years when I clung to the philosophy of economic determinism as an explanation of man's fate, still there were moments when in the midst of misery and class strife, life was shot through with glory. Mrs. Barrett in her sordid little tenement flat finished her breakfast dishes at ten o'clock in the morning and got down on her knees and prayed to God.

The Harrington family also lived in that block of tenements, and there were nine children, the eldest a little girl
of twelve. She was a hard-working little girl, and naturally
I had the greatest admiration for her on account of the
rigorous life she led. I had a longing then, I can remember,
for the rigorous life. I was eight, and I had begun to help
my mother for the first time. It was the first time our own
family (to me a large one though we were only six) had to
do without a servant, and my sister and I were pressed into
service to help with dishes and housecleaning. I remember
the joy I got out of it, this having a part in the family's
concerns, having them depend on me too for my help. I
took my dishwashing very seriously and I can remember
scouring faucets until they shone. The work grew wearisome, of course; it did not always have the aspect of a
game. But it had to be done and after six months of it, I
was well used to the fact that I had to do my share.

But I had a tremendous amount of liberty compared to
little Mary Harrington, my senior. It was not until after
the dishes were done that she could come out to play in
the evening. Often she was so tired that we just stretched
out on the long back porch, open to the sky. We lay there,
gazing up at the only beauty the city had to offer us, and
we talked and dreamed.

I don't remember what we talked about, but I do remember one occasion when she told me of the life of some
saint. I don't know which one nor can I remember any of
the incidents of it. I can only remember the feeling of lofty

enthusiasm I had, how my heart seemed almost bursting with desire to take part in such high endeavor. One verse of the Psalms often comes to my mind: "Enlarge thou my heart, O Lord, that Thou mayest enter in." This was one of those occasions when my small heart was enlarged. I could feel it swelling with love and gratitude to such a good God for such a friendship as Mary's, for conversation such as hers, and I was filled with lofty ambitions to be a saint, a natural striving, a thrilling recognition of the possibilities of spiritual adventure.

I, too, wanted to do penance for my own sins and for the sins of the whole world, for I had a keen sense of sin, of natural imperfection and earthliness. I often felt clearly that I was being deliberately evil in my attitudes, just as I clearly recognized truth when I came across it. And the thrill of joy that again and again stirred my heart when I came across spiritual truth and beauty never abated, never left me as I grew older.

The sad thing is that one comes across it so seldom. Natural goodness, natural beauty, brings joy and a lifting of the spirit, but it is not enough, it is not the same. The special emotions I am speaking of came only at hearing the word of God. It was as though each time I heard our Lord spoken of, a warm feeling of joy filled me. It was hearing of someone you love and who loves you.

Chapter Three

EARLY YEARS

I T SEEMS TO ME as I look back upon it that I had a childhood that was really a childhood and that I was kept in the status of a child until I was sixteen. We had a very close family life. We knew little about community life, however. There was no radio at that time so the news of the world was not blared into the home a dozen times a day. Father was very particular, too, as to what books and magazines were brought into the home. We had Scott, Hugo, Dickens, Stevenson, Cooper, and Edgar Allan Poe. We seldom were allowed to have friends in the house because it interfered with father's privacy.

I am grateful to my mother and father for this sheltered childhood, a disciplined childhood with so few distractions that books were our only release and outlook.

We went to the movies once a week on Sunday afternoons. That was the time of Wild West stories and mystery tales, and though nothing positively good was shown, neither was there anything bad. Whatever I learned of evil came from children I played with rather than from books or movies.

St. Augustine's remarks on childhood help me to remember the feelings and actions of even my earliest youth. I recall stealing when I was about six, not only once but on two separate occasions, and both times I was found out and felt dishonored and full of remorse. But whether the remorse was occasioned by my sin being discovered or by public opinion, I do not remember. I do remember, however, how it ate into my vitals, how I watered my bed with my tears, how disgraced I felt and how black the world seemed to me, laden with guilt as I was. I do not think St. Augustine's words were too strong when he wrote as he did in his confessions.

My mother had great natural virtues and a delightful temperament that helped her through much hardship and uncertainty. She refused to worry when things were going badly, or when the family had its periods of poverty. There were days when she had to do the family washing, the sheets, blankets, and all, and after a day in the basement laundry, she used to bathe and dress as though she were going out to a dinner party.

She reigned over the supper table as a queen, powdered, perfumed, daintily clothed, all for the benefit of us children. She is still a woman who loves people and uses her charm to please them. She loves life and all the gaieties and frivolities of life; but when through poverty she was deprived of "good times" she made them for herself and got enjoyment from little things. When she felt low she used to go downtown and squander a little money, shopping for a bargain in a hat or a new blouse, never forgetting to bring home some little gift for us all.

For me, this childhood was happy in spite of moods of uncertainty and even of hopelessness and sadness. The latter mood only accentuated the joys that were truly there. Yet I knew that this happiness was a matter of temperament and disposition, too, because often on talking over past days with my sister, she could think only of her own moods of misery. From her own account she suffered far more than I ever did. She never had religious moods, she never felt the certainty of the existence of God. She had seen far more of the tragedy of life than I, as one of her school friends had died and for a long time after she was haunted by the fear of death. In all my moods of sadness, the thought of death coming to any of our dear ones never occurred to me. I feared death for myself, but the thought that my mother and my brother might die never entered my mind.

Much as I loved people, they did not make me suffer as they did my sister. My unhappiness always came from within myself. Looking back, I can see that it was not so much evil that I was protected from when the family kept us from shallow books, movies, newspapers, and other outside contacts, as it was that we were saved from the cluttered existence that people led. We were kept from the empty distractions that so many had to offer. We were more alone. Even education at that time was not so crowded.

There were long study periods in school, and we had no homework until high school.

There were long hours and periods when I had nothing to do except what I chose to do. I can remember long, interminable Sunday afternoons, long, even sad, summer afternoons when there was "nothing to do." Friends were away or we were kept in the house by the weather or by illness. And our parents did nothing to offer us distraction or entertainment. We were forced to meet our moods and overcome them. We were forced even to find tasks for ourselves, which may have been a good thing.

There were times when my sister and I turned to housework from very boredom. But those mornings when we awoke with a firm determination to turn to good account the daylight hours, when we scrubbed porches, swept the long rooms, and settled down to leisure in the afternoon over a book or a piece of writing, will ever stand out in my mind. There was time to think, to think about fundamental things.

A mood which came to me again and again after some happiness or triumph was one of sadness at the fleeting of human joy. One afternoon, not long after I had won a scholarship of three hundred dollars and knew I was going away to college, I walked the streets at sunset gazing at the clouds over Lincoln Park, recognizing the world as supremely beautiful, yet oppressed somehow with a heavy and abiding sense of loneliness and sadness.

When I was twelve years old an Episcopalian minister, canvassing the neighborhood for his parishioners, came to the house and discovering that my mother had been brought up in that church, persuaded her to send me to the confirmation class that was being started. I had not yet been baptized so as I learned the catechism I was preparing at the same time for confirmation. I cannot remember being particularly affected by these formalities. I went willingly every Monday afternoon because my fourteen-year-old playmate went also. I did not like her especially but she was around our house a great deal. It was for the companionship of my elder brothers. She was a self-conscious, affected girl with a precocious interest in sex. She was a most unwholesome companion but none of our elders suspected it because her manners were pretty and she was always most respectful to them.

The godparents that were picked out for me were two parishioners, mother and son, whom I had never known before and whose names I do not recall now. I remember being much embarrassed at being baptized, tall, gawky girl that I was, and the fact that I was one of many being confirmed did not make me feel any easier. Going to the communion rail was an agony. Fortunately one did not have to do that more than a few times a year. What I did love were the Psalms and anthems, the rubrics of the church. When the choir sang the *Te Deum* or the *Benedicite* my heart melted within me. They expressed pure truth and beauty to me, and for a year or so I never missed Sunday service.

You, younger brother, were born when I was fourteen years old and the two years after were years of discipline for me. Up to that time my life had been a free one; but now mother was not so strong and much of the care of you devolved upon Grace and me. We were living, at that time, on the North side of Chicago near Lincoln Park in a house that was a delight to us. Our life up to then had been one of constant change. We had moved from New York to Berkeley, to Oakland, to Chicago; and in Chicago, we had moved four times. We children had attended about six schools. We had lived in houses and apartments, and none of them meant anything to us.

But the house that we were living in at that time did. There were large rooms, and the living room on the first floor had steps going up through it to the bedrooms upstairs. There was a grate fireplace in that living room and bookcases on either side. Carpet covered the parlor, the living room, the hall, and the stairs, a heavy brown carpet with black figures in it, and that carpet had to be swept every Saturday morning. Grace began upstairs in the halls and swept down, while I began at the front door and swept back. It took hours. It was back-breaking work, that wielding of brooms, before the day of the vacuum cleaner. We did not have electricity in the house — only gas. But we loved the house so we loved the work. That house to us was "home."

34

There was a round table in the center of the living room with a heavy cloth on it. Around the table were four or five comfortable chairs. On the center of the table was a green-shaded gas lamp that always leaked a little. Every night we sat there, my brothers, my mother, Grace, and I, and read before going to bed. There was sociability at meals but those hours in the evening were always given up to reading and no one was allowed to talk and violate that quiet.

Father was never home evenings because he was working nights on the *Inter Ocean*. The others went to bed before I did, but I stayed up as late as I liked, which was sometimes very late indeed. Mother knew that I knew that I had to get up around four with you when you first started chirping with the birds, so she trusted to my own good sense to get enough sleep. But I was in love with the hard life, then, and sat up, until after midnight, reckless of my strength.

I had a special seat by the fire with a pile of books beside me. It was never one book that engrossed me but a dozen. I was hungry for knowledge and had to devour volumes. In school I was studying Latin and Greek, history and English, and there was a good deal of homework. But I never thought of homework in the evening — those were my hours of freedom. In the cellar was a barrel of apples and we used to bring up a plate of them. I always peeled mine and ate them with salt as I read.

De Quincey was my favorite author, and I read everything he wrote that I could get from the library. Spencer was another writer that I tried hard to read. I wanted to read him because I came across references to his work in Jack London's books. Of course I read everything of Jack London's and Upton Sinclair's, and they had much influence on my way of thinking. With it all I still read Wesley, the New Testament and *The Imitation of Christ,* and received great comfort from them.

How blessed was sleep after those late hours of reading! On cold winter nights how chilly was the bedroom upstairs in the back of the house, and how warm the bed, warmed by Grace for some hours before I got into it. If I said a prayer at all, I probably fell asleep in the middle of it. I was so starved for sleep those days.

The hours in the afternoon were lovely ones, though I was often tired and dazed from lack of sleep. But I wandered along the paths, pushing your carriage, watching the changing seasons through summer and late fall and winter, happy in the beauty of the trees and the lake which changed from day to day. Sometimes Grace came with me and we talked for hours about the books we were reading, what we wanted to do and couldn't do, of all our half-formulated dreams and desires. But more often she was at home helping mother around the house, and those hours were mine, with you before me in the carriage, to dream of what I was reading and of the evening before me.

When what I read made me particularly class-conscious, I used to turn from the park with all its beauty and peacefulness and walk down to North Avenue and over West through slum districts, and watch the slatternly women and the unkempt children and ponder over the poverty of the homes as contrasted with the wealth along the shore drive. I wanted even then to play my part. I wanted to write such books that thousands upon thousands of readers would be convinced of the injustice of things as they were. I wanted to do something toward making a "new earth wherein justice dwelleth."

I didn't leave home until you were two and yet with the intense love I bore you, I do not remember once trying to teach you your prayers. You were a precocious baby and could talk early, but I never told you about God. We ourselves were not taught our prayers, so it did not occur to me to teach you. I must have thought, coming from the agnostic household I did, that religion was a private affair, that some people had faith and others didn't. As a matter of fact, I don't remember thinking much about it at all.

I left the Episcopalian church at this time quite definitely. Mother had taken up Christian Science to help herself, perhaps, and because I was suffering from bad headaches at the time, she had treatments for me too. There was a practitioner living across the street and I read *Science and Health* and some of the pamphlets and this new revelation seemed as convincing to me as the dogmas of the Episcopalian church.

The pastor of the church where I had been baptized two years before came to struggle for my soul and remained talking to me all one afternoon, but I was obdurate in my refusal to return to church. I was in a "free" mood and my reading at the time made me skeptical. My belief in God remained firm and I continued to read the New Testament regularly, but I felt it was no longer necessary to go to church. I distrusted all churches after reading the books of London and Sinclair. So from that time on I ceased going, much to the relief of my sister who complained when I dragged her unwillingly to services.

Chapter Four

COLLEGE

I WAS SIXTEEN when I graduated from high school and went to the University of Illinois. It was in 1914 and that summer the war had broken out in Europe. It was talked about along Webster Avenue where we lived and it was felt by all our neighbors, many of whom were Germans, but I was not affected by it in any way. The world could be convulsed with struggle, unhappiness and misery could abound on every side, but I was supremely happy. I was leaving home for the first time. Things were happening. I was going away to school. I was grown up.

But after those first glowing weeks of happiness I suffered miserably. I suffered because I was separated from you. It was as though I had been torn from my own child. After I was settled at the Y.W.C.A., after I had registered for classes, after I had found work to supplement the money I had in the bank to make it last as long as possible, instead of settling down to happiness in my work, I settled down to a dull, plodding misery.

For the first time in my life I suffered from insomnia. No matter how late I stayed up, trying to study, I could not sleep. Hour after hour I lay awake, thinking of home and of you, and how you must miss me as I missed you. Everything was cold and dead to me. I wanted the warmth of my home, I wanted my own, and I felt utterly abandoned. I was so completely homesick that I could neither eat nor sleep, and I paced the brick-paved walks of that small college town with tears streaming down my face, my heart so heavy that it hung like a weight in my breast.

Fortunately I had much work to do. That first semester I worked for my board with a professor who taught romance languages. I had breakfast at the "Y" but at lunch time I went to Professor Fitzpatrick's and had lunch with his family that consisted of his wife, mother, and three children. They were Methodists and pious people and I used to talk about faith with the old lady as she washed the lunch dishes and prepared vegetables for the evening meal.

But even as I talked about religion, I didn't like church. I grew to dislike hymn singing and I didn't like the people who went in for both. I was repelled by them. I disliked them and did not want to be like them. As a matter of fact, I started to swear, quite consciously began to blaspheme in order to shock them. I shocked myself as I did it. I had to practice it in order to become used to it, but I felt that it was a strong gesture I was making to push religion from me. It certainly was a most conscious gesture. Because I was unhappy, I felt harsh. Because I was hurt at being torn from you, my child and my brother, I had to turn away from home and faith and all the gentle things of life and seek the hard. In spite of my studies and my work, I had time to read, and the ugliness of life in a world which professed itself to be Christian appalled me.

Now I was away from home, living my own life, and I had to choose the world to which I wanted to belong. I most decidedly did not want to belong to the Epworth League. As a little child the happy peace of the Methodists who lived next door appealed to me deeply. Now that same happiness seemed to be a smug disregard of the misery of the world, a self-satisfied consciousness of being saved.

While I was going to school that year, my oldest brother, just two years older than I, went to work on *The Day Book*, a small, ad-less newspaper, an experiment in journalism, which was being published then in Chicago. Carl Sandburg, the poet, worked on it and many Socialists. Because it was radical, it was considered to be socialistic, but I do not know if it was politically. My memory may be at fault but it seems to me that it was an experiment of Scripps-Howard or a son of one or the other. Because they did not take advertising from the department stores, they were free to criticize wages and hours and conditions of labor in the department stores, and my brother used to send me the papers daily with his stories marked in them.

While I was free to go to college, I was mindful of girls working in stores and factories through their youth and afterward married to men who were slaves in those same factories.

41

The Marxist slogan, "Workers of the world unite, you have nothing to lose but your chains," seemed to me a most stirring battle cry, and it was to me a clarion call that made me feel one with the masses, apart from the bourgeoisie, the smug, and the satisfied.

The romanticism and the hardness of Jack London in his stories of the road appealed to me more at that time than the idealism of Upton Sinclair, though I still considered, and do yet to this day, that *The Jungle* was a great novel. But his romantic, realistic novel, *The Mystery of Love,* repelled me so that I discounted his other books. He had not yet written his other great labor novels which are superior to anything London wrote.

The Russians appealed to me, too, and I read everything of Dostoevsky that I could lay my hands on, as well as the novels of Artzybashev, Andreyev, Chekhov, Turgenev, Gorki, and Tolstoi. Both Dostoevsky and Tolstoi made me cling to a faith in God, and yet I could not endure feeling so alone in it. I felt that my faith had nothing in common with that of Christians around me.

It seems to me that I was already shedding it when a professor whom I much admired made a statement in class — I shall always remember it — that religion was something which had brought great comfort to people throughout the ages, so that we ought not to criticize it. I do not remember his exact words, but from the way he spoke of religion the class could infer that the strong were the ones who did not need such props. In my youthful arrogance, in my feeling

42

that I was one of the strong, I felt then for the first time that religion was something that I must ruthlessly cut out of my life.

Just recently I read a revolutionary novel, *Bread and Wine* by Ignazio Silone, and this passage struck my eyes so that I copied it out. It is not Catholic doctrine and I do not subscribe to it, but it does remind me of how I felt at that time.

"I lost my faith in God many years ago," the young man said, and his voice changed. "It was a religious impulse that led me into revolutionary movement, but once within the movement, I gradually rid my head of all religious prejudices. If any traces of religion are left in me, they are not a help but a hindrance to me now. Perhaps it was the religious education I received as a boy that made me a bad revolutionary, a revolutionary full of fears, uncertainties and complexities. On the other hand, should I ever have become a revolutionary without it? Should I ever have taken life seriously?"

The old priest smiled.

"It does not matter," he said. "In times of conspiratorial and secret struggle, the Lord is obliged to hide Himself and assume pseudonyms. Besides, and you know it, He does not attach very much importance to His name. On the contrary, at the very beginning of His commandments he ordained that His name should not be taken in vain. Might not the ideal of social justice that animates the masses today be one of the pseudonyms the Lord is using to free Himself from the control of the churches and the banks?"

"There is an old story that must be called to mind every time the existence of God is doubted," he went on. "It is written, perhaps you will remember, that at the moment of a great distress Elijah asked the Lord to let him die, and the Lord summoned him to a mountain, and there arose a great and mighty wind that struck the mountain and split the rocks, but the Lord was not in the wind. And after the wind, the earth was shaken by an earthquake, but the Lord was not in the earthquake. And after the earthquake there arose a great fire, but the Lord was not in the fire. But afterwards in the silence, there was a still, small voice, like the whisper of branches moved by an evening breeze, and that still small voice, it is written, was the Lord."

So I felt at the time that religion would only impede my work. I wanted to have nothing to do with the religion of those whom I saw all about me. I felt that I must turn from it as from a drug. I felt it indeed to be an opiate of the people, so I hardened my heart.

It was a conscious and deliberate process, helped along by everything that I read. It needed cataclysms, it needed mighty winds, it needed the silence of mountain tops in my life to enable me to hear the still small voice of God. And my life was beginning to be full and busy and overladen with new impressions and emotions.

My work kept me from mingling much with other students the first five months I was away at the University of Illinois. I was greedy for the books that money could buy and I spent all my spare hours working to earn the money for them. In addition to working for my board, I took two-hour jobs washing and ironing clothes and taking care of children. The latter job was easy because it meant long evening hours to read.

It doesn't seem to me that I put in much time studying. I was taking history, biology, Latin, and English, but nothing that I studied was related to life as I saw it. Even history did not teach me to study past events in relation to present ones with the intention of shaping the present to mould the future. I was not interested in biology so I skipped courses recklessly. I had loved the hours spent in reading Virgil in high school, and was so enamored of his verse that I went from the *Aeneid* to his *Eclogues* and *Bucolics,* reading them for my own pleasure at home. But I lost interest in Latin at college. The only thing I was really interested in was reading the books I selected for myself, and, of course, writing.

Before the two years were up, I had exhausted the money I had and many times I was out of work and money. To gain more time to read and write, I took a room in the home of a poverty-stricken instructor who had five children. I did not eat with them — they had scarcely enough for themselves — but I earned my room by doing the family washing on Saturdays. Many a time I scrubbed the skin off my knuckles laundering the baby clothes, and my back ached for days from the Saturday toil over the washtub and ironing board. I earned my room but to get money for my board it was necessary to take at least a two-hour job a day that would bring me forty cents. Forty cents a day would do me for food if I bought it myself and cooked over a one-burner oil stove. But my critical attitude toward the "Y," which controlled the employment bureau, and my godless spirits kept me from getting many jobs. Besides, I got immersed in writing and let days go by without working so that I went hungry.

I really led a very shiftless life, doing for the first time exactly what I wanted to do, attending only those classes I wished to attend, coming and going at whatever hour of the night I pleased. My freedom intoxicated me. I felt it was worth going hungry for.

I got some work writing for space rates on the little town paper and occasionally it published a column. Many of my columns were critical of the existing order and those were not published. Some of the columns merely criticized the working conditions of the students and these were published which got me in some hot water. I do not think I was very well liked.

I had joined a little club for writers and the first story I turned in was on the experience of going hungry. It was not a bid for pity. I had taken a grim satisfaction at being made to pay the penalty for my own non-conformity, and I wrote with a great relish of three days without other food than salted peanuts. I knew of several jobs I could have taken, one of them with a bootlegger's family in Urbana, the adjoining town, taking care of a howling troupe of children, which would have brought me money for food. But I had spent a week there and the sordid dreariness of the surroundings, the unattractive children, the unsavory character of my employer, had repelled me so that I left and took the room in the instructor's household.

The room was bare and carpetless. There was a bed, a table, and chair, and the little stove to cook what food I had. My books were piled on the floor. It was cold so that it was hard to study at night. Even in bed it was impossible to keep warm. The winds from the prairie howled into the shabby old house and the heavy snows and sleet beat against the window. At night I could study in the university library. When I went back to my room I had to go to bed immediately, and when I was cold and hungry it was hard to get up in the morning. If it had not been for my English classes which I really enjoyed, I should have given up classes and stayed in bed for days. I was seventeen, and I felt completely alone in the world, divorced from family, from all security, even from God. I felt a sense of reckless arrogance and with this recklessness, I felt a sense of danger and rejoiced in it. It was good to live dangerously.

There was no one to guide my footsteps to the paths of the Spirit, and everything I read turned me away from it. The call to my youth was the call of Kropotkin, and the beauty of his prose, the nobility of his phrasing, appealed to my heart. He wrote in his appeal to youth:

If you reason instead of repeating what is taught you; if you analyze the law and strip off those cloudy fictions with which it has been draped in order to conceal its real origin, which is the right of the tyrannies handed down to mankind through its long and bloody history; when you have comprehended this, your contempt for the law will be very profound indeed. You will understand that to remain the servant of the written law is to place yourself every day in opposition to the law of conscience, and to make a bargain on the wrong side; and since this struggle cannot go on forever, you will either silence your conscience and become a scoundrel, or you will break with tradition, and you will work with us for the utter destruction of all this injustice, economic, social and political. But then you will be a Revolutionist.

Two courses are open to you: You can either tamper forever with your conscience and finish one day by saying, humanity can go to the devil as long as I am enjoying every pleasure to the full and so long

48

as the people are foolish enough to let me do so. Or else you will join the ranks of the revolutionists and work with them for the complete transformation of society. Such is the necessary results of the analysis we have made; such is the logical conclusion at which every intelligent being must arrive, provided he judge impartially the things he sees around him, and disregards the sophism suggested to him by his middle-class education and the interested views of his friends.

Having once reached this conclusion the question which arises is, What is to be done? The answer is easy.

Quit the environment in which you are placed and in which it is customary to speak of the workers as a lot of brutes. Be amongst the people, and the question will solve itself.

This was Kropotkin, to me at that time a saint in his way.

Whatever I had read as a child about the saints had thrilled me. I could see the nobility of giving one's life for the sick, the maimed, the leper. Priests and Sisters the world over could be working for the littlest ones of Christ, and my heart stirred at their work. Who could hear of Damien — and Stevenson made the whole world hear of him — without feeling impelled to thank God that he had made man so noble?

But there was another question in my mind. Why was so much done in remedying the evil instead of avoiding it in the first place? There were day nurseries for children, for instance, but why didn't fathers get money enough to take care of their families so that the mothers would not have to go out to work? There were hospitals to take care of the sick and infirm, and, of course, doctors were doing much to prevent sickness, but what of occupational diseases, and the diseases which came from not enough food for the mother and children? What of the disabled workers who received no compensation but only charity for the rest of their lives?

Disabled men, men without arms and legs, blind men, consumptive men, exhausted men with all the manhood drained from them by industrialism; farmers gaunt and harried with debt; mothers weighted down with children at their skirts, in their arms, in their wombs, and the children ailing, rickety, toothless — all this long procession of desperate people called to me. Where were the saints to try to change the social order, not just to minister to the slaves but to do away with slavery?

St. Peter said, "Servants, be subject to your masters with all fear, not only to the good and gentle but also to the froward" (1 Pet. 2:18). And the Socialists said, "Workers of the world unite, you have nothing to lose but your chains."

Our Lord said, "Blessed are the meek," but I could not be meek at the thought of injustice. I wanted a Lord who would scourge the money lenders out of the temple, and

I wanted to help all those who raised their hand against oppression.

Religion, as it was practiced by those I encountered (and the majority were indifferent), had no vitality. It had nothing to do with everyday life; it was a matter of Sunday praying. Christ no longer walked the streets of this world, He was two thousand years dead and new prophets had risen up in His place.

I was in love with the masses. I do not remember that I was articulate or reasoned about this love, but it warmed my heart and filled it. It was those among the poor and the oppressed who were going to rise up, they were collectively the new Messiah, and they would release the captives. Already they had been persecuted, they had been scourged, they had been thrown into prison and put to death, not only all over the world but right around me in the United States.

There were the I.W.W.'s throughout the West, Bill Haywood, Elizabeth Gurley Flynn, Arturo Giovannitti, and Carlo Tresca. There were the Haymarket martyrs who had been "framed" and put to death in Chicago. They were martyrs. They had died for a cause. Even Judge Gary admitted that. In his charge to the jury he had said, "The conviction had not gone on the ground that they did actually have any personal participation in that particular act, but the conviction proceeds upon the ground that they had generally by speech and spirit, advised large classes of people, not particular individuals but large classes, to commit murder...and in consequence of that advice and influenced by that advice, somebody not known, did throw this bomb." This incitement, according to Lucy Parsons, widow of one of the martyrs, writing in a bitter letter to a labor newspaper years after, consisted in their appeal to workers to organize for the eight-hour day.

There had been in the past the so-called Molly Maguires in the coal fields and the Knights of Labor working for the eight-hour day and the cooperative system. My heart thrilled at those unknown women in New England who led the first strikes to liberate the women and children from the cotton mills.

My mother, now that she saw my interest, told me how she had worked in a shirt factory in Poughkeepsie when she was a girl. She had seen no romance, no interest in those few hard years of her life, until she saw it through my eyes. As a matter of fact, to her it was one of those episodes to be forgotten.

Already in this year 1915 great strides had been taken. In some places the ten-hour day and increased wages had been won. But still only about eight per cent of the workers were organized, and the great mass of workers throughout the country were ground down by poverty and insecurity. What work there was to be done!

There was a small group of Socialists in the town of Urbana and I joined the party, but the meetings were dull and I didn't attend very many. I was going to turn to larger fields as soon as I could get away from school.

Chapter Five

RAYNA PROHME

J UST LAST WINTER I gave you a book to read, *Personal
History* by Vincent Sheean, and in that book is a chapter called "Revolution." Mostly that chapter is the story of
Rayna Prohme who has fascinated all who read the book.
Of all the people Sheean writes about, she stands out clear,
beautiful, and rare, a character one meets but once in a life-
time. You met her, but you do not remember it. I brought
her home with me to meet the family that first summer
vacation, but you were only three then.

I saw her first on the train going down to the university
in September. She was the one person I remember on the
train filled with students going back to school. She stood
out like a flame with her red hair, brown eyes, and vivid
face. She had a clear, happy look, the look of an honest
and sincere person. She was two or three years older than
I, and was entering her sophomore year then. I was not to
meet her until later that first year.

Her father, I believe, had been president of the Board of
Trade in Chicago and her family was wealthy. She had fallen
in love in high school with a young Jew born on Chrystie

Street on the East Side of New York, who was living during his high school years with relatives in Chicago. She herself was a Jew and her family opposed the marriage because of her youth and his poverty, and wanting to be near him she had gone to the state university so that she could live away from home.

In spite of brilliant scholarship, an outstanding personality, good looks, and wealth, she was not invited to belong to any sorority, and with others of her faith she lived in a rooming house on the edge of the campus. It was the first time I came up against anti-Semitism.

The only benefits those two years at college brought me were my friendship with Rayna and my own sense of complete independence. It was at the time when I was going hungry and becoming increasingly unpopular that I first met her.

There were not more than a dozen people in the writing club I had joined and Rayna and Raph, the boy to whom she was engaged, had been going over the stories turned in for the college magazine when they came across mine. You remember, it was the story on going hungry. Rayna was enthusiastic and we felt we knew each other immediately. The first night we met, the three of us went to a restaurant and sat over coffee for hours. Rayna herself did not write, but Raph did, and she was an energetic critic.

I do not know what her ambition was at that time, if she had any. She was in love and she saw things through Raph's eyes. Or rather she did the studying, the thinking, and tried to guide his thought. Everything she did was for him, and she poured her glowing love out upon him, and all the wealth of her mind and heart. He writes Broadway plays now and has a yacht and a penthouse apartment. But that is not what she wanted for him. She was avid for knowledge and for beauty, and what she wanted him to be was a great novelist who would increase the world's store of beauty.

She was not particularly interested in the social problem then, nor was she for many years. In the light of the story told in *Personal History* it is interesting to think of her as she was when I knew her.

The joy and happiness of those days is still with me. We took long walks over the prairie. We picnicked with our books and a phonograph, playing some Beethoven symphony under the limitless sky while the smell of sweet clover filled the air and the meadow larks pierced the quiet with their songs. And now her dust, in an urn, reposes in Moscow, and I alone pray for her soul, for I am the only one she knew who has a faith in the resurrection of the body and the life everlasting.

Rayna used to laugh at my absorption in Socialism. She felt that I was unbalanced on the subject and was looking at life from only one angle. She thought, too, emotional creature that she was, that my interest was too emotional and not founded upon solid knowledge and she used to urge me to study philosophy and psychology. But I was interested in facts, not speculation. Rayna insisted upon my coming to live with her.

Do you remember in *David Copperfield* your own sense of gratitude to Aunt Betsy for taking David in and feeding him and sheltering him? You should feel grateful to Rayna in the same way. It had been a hard life I was leading. I had not had enough food or sleep for a long time and I had become morbid. Though I rejoiced in my sufferings, taking a grim pleasure in them, I took that pleasure defensively. I built up a consciously dramatic attitude to keep myself from becoming crushed. I was defiant so that I should not own myself beaten or frightened by life.

If I had conformed, I could have had easy jobs, such a job as clerk in the office of the registrar, for instance — neat, orderly jobs. If I had been the good student that I was in high school, I would have had my way made easy for me. One girl I knew gained an instructor's job after two years in the university. I knew that I could have made my way safe and secure, but that was not what I wanted. I was not merely perverse and undisciplined; I was choosing another way, I thought, and since I deliberately chose it, I had no right to regard my poverty or my hardships as other than of my own choosing.

But just the same I had suffered. Rayna took me in. She paid room rent for me out of her allowance. Her family insisted that she take a pint of cream a day, for she was a fragile creature and all her glowing vitality was of the spirit. She made me drink that cream with her, trying to put some flesh on my bones. We ate together at the rooming house table, or we ate out at restaurants. What was hers was also mine, and we loved each other.

I scarcely remember what we read or what we talked about. I remember Rose Pastor Stokes coming to lecture at the school and Rayna and Raph, who worked on the college paper, interviewed her. I remember the argument about what to print and what trouble they would encounter printing all that Mrs. Stokes said. Raph would not print it, nor would the editor, much as they believed in all Mrs. Stokes had to say about the capitalist system and birth control, which she claimed "the system" fought in order to keep the worker oppressed, in order to have more cannon fodder.

We were fascinated by Mrs. Stokes who was from the East Side as Raph was, a factory girl married to a millionaire whom she met during a strike in New York years before. We were excited by the romance of her life as well as by her vivid personality.

Neither of us having any contact with Catholicism or its teaching, we knew of no arguments at all against birth control.

Prominent Socialists, Scott Nearing amongst them, lectured at the university and we met them. John Masefield came and lectured haltingly and we read all his poems. *Spoon River Anthology* had just been published and everybody did imitations of the verse of Edgar Lee Masters. Vachel Lindsay was another favorite and Carl Sandburg.

Some of those Sundays when we went out on the prairie to picnic we took volumes of poetry with us and Rayna read aloud. She herself was poetry to us, both Raph and I loved her so. Not all our discussions were just in the realm of ideas. We were girls, Rayna and I, and much interested in clothes. I had one suit and two blouses, and one silk crepe dress which shrank so when I washed it myself that I could no longer wear it. Rayna had lovely things and used to insist (she did not have to insist very hard) that I borrow them those evenings when we went to the International Club. I was "going with" a young Spaniard whose name I cannot even remember. I liked Raph far better, seeing him through Rayna's eyes.

Later, when I was in Chicago, I saw her only occasionally because she was taking post-graduate courses in the University of Chicago and I was working nights in a print shop. After I left school, she came to New York and spent a summer with me. She and Raph already had discovered that theirs had been a school time love and they separated, he to work on Broadway and she to go back to her academic life. I felt that she was burying herself and she felt that I was throwing myself away. Actually she spent years of study before she met the Communist who later became her husband.

Vincent Sheean has brought out many of her qualities in his picture of her. He has told of their days and nights of conversations both in Hankow where he met her and in Moscow. She was doing an editing job on a Communist newspaper when they met and must have been twenty-seven at the time.

Some years later I learned that she had died, and I felt that a dearly loved friend from whom I had been separated, had gone out of my life for good. It was just as I was becoming a Catholic that she was becoming a Communist in China. Her work there was with Madame Sun Yat-sen and with Borodin, and after the Communist regime in Hankow broke down, she escaped with Madame Sun Yat-sen.

Sheean brings out her bravery and her courage which was of the spirit and strong as death. She was certainly not a creature without imagination, so she must have shrunk in the flesh from the prospect of what might overtake her and those other Communists with whom she worked if she did not succeed in escaping. I wish I knew more of the details of that flight from the conquered city. Sheean himself just gives a bare outline.

He saw her again in Moscow and characteristically she was about to take courses in the Lenin Institute to prepare herself to become a propagandist for worldwide work. It was then, a few weeks after he saw her again, that she suddenly was stricken and died of cerebral hemorrhage. His story of her last days and the account of that Red funeral and the procession in the rain to the crematorium is heartrending.

I tell you all this, though you have read the book, because Sheean brings out two outstanding traits in her character which made so great an impression on me that

I can never forget them. One was her joyousness and the other her love of truth. She had those qualities when he met her. He speaks with love of the way she used to laugh with him over all the incongruities and inconsistencies of their surroundings. It was pure joy that made her laugh with such heartiness.

I remember writing once that joy always brought laughter to me. The sound of a Bach prelude on the university organ as we played hockey on the field in back of the big auditorium; the crowing of a baby; the sight of dolphins leaping through the water alongside of a ship on my way to Florida — these are things I remember off-hand that brought such joy to my heart that I had to laugh as a release, as an expression of that joy in my heart.

Rayna's joyousness came because she saw always what was noble and beautiful in life and she was happy in it. And I can see now, how being a Communist brought out this spirit in her even more.

Her other trait that Sheean emphasized was her love of truth and I am sure that it was that love which, if she had lived, would have forced her to give up the Communist Party. He told that when he was interviewing her she expressed her great distaste for the "lying" that Communist propaganda makes necessary. She told him that when she could not tell the truth, she preferred to remain silent. I do not think she would have made a very good propagandist, no matter how many years she spent in the Lenin

Institute. What I wish to bring out is the positiveness of these virtues, these natural virtues.

Most young people think of virtue as something negative. They think that by avoiding sin they are being good. They think of purity as an absence of impurity. They have not committed those sins which they might have committed. Yet we should think certainly of purity as a shining positive virtue, rather than as a negative one — one that makes itself felt, that stands out glowingly.

It is the Old Testament that emphasizes the "Thou shalt not's." The New Testament emphasizes the positive virtue of love which comprises all the rest.

Have you not met in your life people who stood out because some virtue shone in them, was predominant? I can remember people whose goodness shone as a positive adornment, which attracted others and filled them with longing. It would be so easy for us if there were more to inspire us as they do.

Rayna's truth stood out as a positive virtue. She was honest, pure, and loving, but above all shone her joyousness and her truth.

Catholics who read this may be surprised at this glowing appraisal of one who did not believe in Christ. I must remind them that in spite of living in the United States, in a so-called Christian nation, there were no Christians whom Rayna met who could induce her, either by their actions or their words, to believe in the way of the Cross, in the glorified Christ.

Nothing in her reading that was abstruse and philosophical in school brought her the truth. She was hungering for it, she loved it, she searched for it in years of study at the University of Illinois, but she never found it. She thought she had found it in Communism, then she died. And who knows but that just at death she did find it? We cannot tell. She was searching for it.

I thought of Rayna and the appeal Communism made to her when I read those lines of Maritain:

> The Russian Communists have clearly appreciated those truths (the necessity of reviving the moral ideas that govern the life of the social body as such). They have even formed their party into a kind of brotherhood with an exacting and rigorous discipline, and by every means in their power they endeavor to renew after their fashion the moral bases of life of the whole people, so that what gives their materialist and atheist revolution the deepest power of attracting the souls of men... is the indestructible spiritual appeal (unconfessed because it is not in accordance with the Marxian table of values) of justice, and poverty, of fortitude in suffering.

I always felt that Rayna had those reserves of "spiritual energy" which Maritain speaks of. "It is to be noted," he writes, "that the reserves of spiritual energy that are to be found in human nature may be liberated by preaching and example and set in operation in the hearts of many without any sense of spiritual things other than that which they may find in the concrete experience of the fight for justice here below. . . . "

"It follows from the idea of Catholicity that every just man of non-Christian denomination belongs to the invisible unity of the Church and on this ground only has a title to salvation. . . . "

So reading, my heart is comforted about Rayna, for most assuredly she loved truth and justice.

Chapter Six

NEW YORK

I N JUNE 1916, I left the University of Illinois for good. I had been there for two years and to this day I haven't the slightest idea what I learned in classes. All my education had come from outside.

The family was moving to New York again. We had all been born there except the youngest, and we had been ten years away. In a few months I would be eighteen. I lived at home while I was looking for a job but as soon as I found one that autumn on the *New York Call*, the Socialist paper, I left to take a room down on the East Side.

Up to that time, I had been imbued to some extent by a Messianic idea of the masses, but at that time I was filled with a morbid pity for those who lived in slums. All that summer I was in a state of depression, as I walked the streets of New York making up my mind what to do, where to live.

In the first place I felt unbearably lonesome. Not that I wanted to stay at the University, but I missed my companions, my friendship with Rayna Prohme. She had been the first real friend I had ever had, and we had shared everything with each other for the last year. Now I was alone.

There was no one to talk to, no one to take walks with and discuss problems of the world. I had grown away from the family and after my crowded life at the university, New York was a vast wilderness.

For weeks I was oppressed by the misery of human existence. The people I saw in subways, in crowded eating places, walking the streets, sitting on park benches, or looking for work, all seemed miserable and hopeless. The city was unbearably hot and airless. For days it seemed that I talked to no one. I walked the streets in solitude and my heart wept within me for the ugliness of all I saw. I could not but believe that all whom I met were as miserable as I.

When I was in the subway I felt closed in, trapped. When I walked the narrow streets of lower New York through the tenement districts I felt that I was caught, that never again would I feel happy or free. It was hot that year and children slept on fire escapes and roofs, and men and women sat on the streets all night. People lived in the streets; and the foul odor of decaying garbage, the fetid odor from the dark hallways of tenements, sickened me. "Where youth grows pale and specter thin and dies," I thought, remembering a poem Rayna and I had read together, "Where but to think is to be full of sorrow and leaden-eyed despair."

As soon as I got work on *The Call,* I went down Pearl Street where I worked, down Cherry Street, and walked up and down tenement stairs investigating the furnished room signs. There were not many of them, for the tenement apartments were small, some even two-room flats. I came across backyard houses, shut in between the high walls of warehouses and factories and other tenements. I came across many a house with backyard toilets.

Cherry Street is a street of "homes," not of rooming houses. There are Syrian, Italian, Greek, and Jewish stores, and the room I finally found was in the home of a Jewish family.

The hallways were dark and evil smelling. There were tile floors, usually slimy with filth. The hallways were narrow with a door on either side opening into the front apartments. At the dusky end of the hall were two more doors entering the rear apartments. The stairs led up for five flights with windows looking out into areaways. The apartment where I found a room was on the fourth floor, front. There were three rooms to the apartment, only the front room with windows on the street.

The front room was used as dining room and bedroom as well as living room, and the kitchen also had folding beds in it. I had the one bedroom with a little gas plate, which I bought myself on which to cook breakfast. There was a bed with an enormous feathertick on top of it, a table, and a chair. These filled the room. There were two doors, one into the kitchen and the other into the hallway. There was one window looking out on an airshaft, but because there was only one flight above, my room was light. I could lie in bed and gaze up at a little patch of sky.

In the two front rooms lived a tailor and his wife and four children. For my bedroom I paid five dollars a month, and probably the rent of the place was ten dollars for the family. There was no electricity, no bath, no hot water, but the children and the mother and father were always clean, thanks to the public showers around the corner, and the place was always neat and smelled of good baking.

The tenement was only one of the thousands in the city. Laws had been passed twenty-five years before condemning them, still they remained, the owners not much concerned about the misery of the occupants.

The fire escapes were obsolete, the windows were too small. Doors, hallways, and stairs were wooden, and every winter there were fires in which men, women, and children lost their lives. There was no central heating. Every family had to heat its own apartment. In some families where the men were employed they used coal. In other families the younger boys would go down to the river and fish up driftwood for the fires.

Some families used their gas ovens for a few hours or just trusted to the gas heat from cooking to warm their homes. Some big tenements had been remodeled to the extent of putting in hot water but not heat. I lived in one such house once, and the family next door used to draw their washtubs full of hot water the first thing in the morning, hoping that the steam would take the chill off the place. Most of the kitchens had two washtubs next to the sink with the partitions between them taken out so as to form one long bathtub.

When the apartments were cold they smelled dank. There was a peculiar odor of burned grease and of dirty clothes. And of course there were bedbugs. I complained quite a few times until I realized what a hopeless struggle it was.

The Call was a morning paper, so I never got to my room until two or three in the morning. Mrs. Gottlieb used to try to keep the children quiet in the morning so that I could sleep, but by nine o'clock they were snuffling around the door waiting for me to waken. I had a portable phonograph that was a great attraction to them, and every morning while I dressed I used to put on a Fritz Kreisler record and I could hear the audience buzzing outside the door like a hive of bees. As soon as I opened the door, they came swarming in to sit all over the bed and the floor while I made myself a pot of coffee. Sometimes Mrs. Gottlieb and the children and I would go together to the public baths around the corner and luxuriate under the hot showers.

My salary in the beginning was five dollars a week. Within a few months it was raised to ten. My rent was only five dollars a month, and I cooked breakfast in my room. Some of the reporters from other papers with whom I was covering assignments used to treat me to dinner, and Mrs. Gottlieb left a plate of soup or fish for me at midnight so that I fared very well.

I have learned since that the poverty of the East Side is comparatively well-fed poverty. There are always the push-cart markets with all kinds of fruits and vegetables. Mussels were the cheapest of the sea foods, and you could buy a leg of chicken and cook up a pot of soup. The Jews and Italians knew how to cook and they did not mind haggling at the push-carts over pennies.

On the East Side both Jews and Italians joined in constant protest against their lot. There were constant bread riots that winter with mobs of women and children storming the city hall. On one occasion they marched up Fifth Avenue to the old Waldorf-Astoria and holding their babies on stout hips, shook their fists up at the windows. They lived on the streets from early spring until late fall and willingly joined in any protest afoot.

There are always protests on the East Side — street corner meetings, marches to the city hall, protests for playgrounds, recreational centers, for babies' clinics, better schools, against low wages, against the high price of living. Usually the protests grew out of some specific case of human misery — death in the family from a fire, starvation, eviction. The family that was suffering sat at home and mourned, and all the neighbors took up the cause and made their voices heard. Consequently, evictions were halted, relief came, playgrounds were built, houses were torn down, and conditions have somewhat improved. But with all the protest there is still no model housing for the very poor. What model tenements have been put up have come to those who could pay thirty to forty dollars a month rent. The poor still live in hovels, paying eight, ten, or fifteen dollars.

I enjoyed that winter in the slums and have never lived any place else since. If one must dwell in cities I prefer the slums of the poor to the slums of the rich. A tenement is a tenement whether it is on lower Park Avenue or upper.

There were several factions working for *The New York Call.* The managing editor, Chester Wright, was an American Federation of Labor man. Charles Ervin, who was on the paper in some business capacity and took Wright's place later as managing editor, favored the Amalgamated Clothing Workers which had had a long fight against the A.F. of L. Joshua Wanhope, the paper's editorial writer, was an old-time Socialist. Most of those working for the paper were Socialists, but there were a few I.W.W.'s and a few Anarchists. Those who favored the I.W.W. or the Anarchist movement, however, were more newspaper men than anything else. Otherwise they could not have worked for *The Call* as Socialism and Anarchism are fundamentally opposed, and the I.W.W.'s, advocating direct action rather than parliamentary action, were disrupters when they were most sincere.

There were two young men that I used to "run around with," William Randorf and Louis Weitzonkorn. They were both radical journalists at the time, but both had their vices which neutralized their work in the movement. Bill's vice was poker and Louis' playwriting. He used to run the

Guillotine Column on *The Call,* and has now become a Broadway playwright, making money and name with *Five Star Final.* Randorf continues to play poker for weeks at a time but has remained to some extent in the radical movement writing labor articles and now and again editing *The Daily Worker.* At that time the three of us were interested in literature as well as labor and journalism and used to sit in Child's restaurant on lower Park Row every morning until two or three o'clock talking about the great novel, the great poem, and the great play. Louis was romantic, and his favorite play was *Cyrano de Bergerac.* He had a big nose himself. Bill's favorite poem was "Cynara."

I was only eighteen, so I wavered between my allegiance to Socialism, Syndicalism (the I.W.W.'s), and Anarchism. When I read Tolstoi I was an Anarchist. My allegiance to *The Call* kept me a Socialist, although a left-wing one, and my Americanism inclined me to the I.W.W. movement.

I do not remember any anti-religious articles in *The Call.* As a matter of fact, there was a long article by Dante Barton, vice-chairman of the Committee on Industrial Relations, which was an interview with Father John O'Rourke, a Jesuit, who preached at the Cathedral that winter. Reading it over just the other day, I was surprised to find many quotations from Pope Leo XIII and a very fair exposition of the Church's social teachings. I had paid no attention to it at that time. Catholics then were a nation apart, a people within a people, making little impression on the tremendous non-Catholic population of the country. The quotations from Father O'Rourke emphasized, as Pope Pius XI did in his encyclical on *Atheistic Communism,* that the bonuses employers handed out were merely bribes. However, at that time as too often even now, social justice was talked of in general principles and not applied to an immediate issue, to any particular strike.

There was little unemployment because the munition factories were working twenty-four hours a day. Although there were high wages, the cost of living went up steadily, so there continued to be strikes in industry. There was a street-car strike which petered out after many months. There were strikes in garment factories, smelting plants, sugar refineries, and week after week during that winter food riots went on. On the west coast Mooney was being tried after the Preparedness Day parade bombing and Bob Minor, the radical cartoonist, was single-handed in building up a defense committee which is still functioning to this day. Charles Ashley, out in Everett, Washington, was doing the same thing for the seventy I.W.W.'s being tried for murder after five of their own comrades had been shot down in a free speech riot. (Now, twenty years after, Minor is still a leader in the Communist labor movement in this country and Ashley is editing a paper in Soviet Russia.)

Chapter Seven

REPORTING

IT WAS DURING the winter of 1916–1917 that I worked on *The Call,* just before the United States declared war. There were the beginnings of a peace movement among students and workers. The Russian Revolution had not yet taken place. Trotsky, exiled from Germany, France, and Spain successively, had come to New York to write on the Russian socialist daily, *Novy Mir.*

The offices of the paper were then at 77 St. Mark's Place, and I went with another *Call* reporter to interview him. He refused to be lured into talking about his exile in Siberia or his various escapes in disguise, but talked instead of the failure of Socialism to halt the war. Perhaps it was his bitter criticism of the parliamentarianism of the Socialists of New York which kept *The Call* from printing more than the one interview with him. His name appeared only twice in the paper.

The Call had been emphasizing constantly the work of the Socialists in the legislature, headlining the activities of Shiplakov and the other Socialists who were prominent in politics. Trotsky said that where parliamentarianism was weakest the Socialistic movement was strongest. Where they sought to win the state, he said, they were won by the state. (His words should be of interest to Catholics who trust to political activity rather than to Catholic action to further the Christian revolution.) Trotsky predicted the ruin of the capitalist class, terrific taxes after the war, and concentration of power in the middle class. "The social unrest," he said, "after the war will eclipse anything the world has ever seen. The workers will take a heavy accounting of masters and the future alone can tell what form the protest will take." A few weeks later he spoke at Cooper Union. "Revolution is brewing in the trenches," he said, little dreaming himself perhaps that on March 21, less than two months later, the New York masses would be celebrating the downfall of the Czar at Madison Square Garden. Ludwig Lore, now a writer for *The Post* and at that time editor of the *Volkzeitung*, introduced his friend.

Life on a newspaper, whether it is a radical or a conservative one, makes one lose all perspective at the time. One is carried along in a world of events, writing, reporting, with no time at all for thought — one day listening to Trotsky and the next day interviewing Mrs. Vincent Astor's butler, writing articles about the Navy Department's charges against Charles Schwab and other munition makers, stories about child labor in rural districts, child labor in the laundries (one fourteen-year-old boy working ninety hours weekly). Nothing stood out in my mind. We worked from twelve noon until twelve at night covering meetings and strikes. We walked on picket lines, we investigated starvation and death in the slums.

Our function as journalists seemed to be to build up a tremendous indictment against the present system, a daily tale of horror which would have the cumulative effect of forcing the workers to rise in revolution. Our editorial heads trusted in legislation, but we young ones believed that nothing could be done except by revolution, by use of force. The old time Socialists with the parliamentarianism that Trotsky condemned trusted to education and legislation to change the social order. The editorials and the leading stories in *The Call* indicated that policy, but they were dull and doctrinaire, and the masses who read the paper could not help but read between the lines the incentive to revolt rather than to sow patiently and build slowly. I know that everything that I wrote, I wrote with the impatience of youth. I was hopeless of gradual change.

On March 21, 1917, at Madison Square Garden, I lived with the others those first days of revolt in Russia and felt the exultation, the joyous sense of victory of the masses as they sang *Ei Uchnjem,* the workman's hymn of Russia which seemed to signify, as *The Call* said the next day, that "like the flow of the river is the progress of human events," and they described the song as a "mystic, gripping melody of struggle, a cry for world peace and human brotherhood."

Only two days later a war-mad audience, led by Elihu Root and Mayor Mitchel, filled Madison Square Garden.

The place was filled not with the working masses — the Jews, the Russians, the Slavs in general who live in the slums of New York — but by home guards, Boy Scouts, naval reserves, militia men. It was almost a social event with limousines pouring out the well-dressed, well-fed coupon clippers, to shout for war so that their investments might be protected.

My work during that winter was to cover strikes, peace meetings, and food riots. Margaret Sanger and her sister, Ethel Byrne, tried to open a birth-control clinic in the slums of Brownsville and were promptly arrested. Ethel Byrne was sent to Blackwell's Island (now called Welfare Island) where she started a hunger strike. It was the first time a woman had ever hunger struck in this country, although the suffragettes in England had used this technique, and the newspapers made much of it. I was assigned to the story, and for the next couple of months my job was to write up these women as martyrs in a holy cause and to paint harrowing pictures of the suffering of Ethel Byrne in jail and after her release. As a matter of fact, she was not on a hunger strike very long. Actually she did not suffer from her hunger strike and she was perfectly well and strong when she was released from jail, a release that was effected by the strike; but my job was to paint a picture of a woman at the point of death. I did not realize until I had been on a hunger strike myself that she was not as weak and ill as she and her doctors claimed, so I wrote the stories as the editor desired them. Just the same, I realized that I was distorting the truth, and it sometimes irked me that my job was always to picture the darker side of life, ignoring all the light touches, the gay and joyful sides of stories as I came across them.

For instance, if I were writing about Mrs. Gottlieb I had to ignore the homely comfort of their well-cooked meals and stress the high cost of living and the insecurity of her husband's employment. I had to leave out the happy pictures of our mornings at the public baths and see only the grim sordidness of the bathless tenement house. I still question the value of this over-emphasis of human misery and under-emphasis of bravery, the courage of human beings enabling them to make the best of their surroundings.

All that winter I enjoyed myself hugely attending labor bazaars and balls given by Socialists, Anarchists, and I.W.W.'s. The most effective speaker I heard was Elizabeth Gurley Flynn who was working with the I.W.W.'s and who was one of the leaders of the strike on the Mesabi iron range. She came to New York to get money for the relief of the miners' families and for labor defense. Wherever she spoke, the audience wept and gave heartily to the cause. The night I heard her she was speaking in the Brownsville section and I gave everything I had in my pocket, not even saving out carfare, so that I had to borrow the fare back to the office and go without lunches for some days afterwards. When I think of the hundreds of meetings I have attended where the workers have contributed toward strikes, labor defense, and the upkeep of their publications I am still amazed at their spirit of sacrifice.

I picketed a good many times that winter in the cold and snow and realized the value of picketing as well as the hardships that go with it. I have spoken many times these last few years to clubs of middle-class women, club women and church women, many among them so ignorant of the labor movement that they had never heard of the American Federation of Labor and did not know what picketing was for. They understood it to be an intimidation, not of strikebreakers, but of the public, and they felt themselves to be brave in going past picket lines into restaurants and stores. They did not realize that this is one way in which the workers can bring their cause to the attention of the public. They did not realize that the industrialists have at their disposal newspapers which are usually on the side of the advertisers, the radio, and very often the pulpit. If they did not picket no one would know that a strike was in progress. Not even other workers who were induced by the offer of higher wages to come and take the jobs, would know that a strike was going on unless they saw a picket line in front of the factory or workshop. I picketed before garment factories and restaurants, and it was hard not only to spend so many hours in an unnaturally slow walk, but it was also hard to face the public and the contempt of most of the police.

By the beginning of March that year students at Columbia became very active in the peace movement and I worked with them, and not only in my role as a reporter. We attended meetings, got out leaflets, and had hundreds of stickers printed protesting the outbreak of war that was imminent. At night we walked together up and down Fifth Avenue, in the subways, and in the department store district and put the stickers on windows and sides of houses. I remember the great enjoyment I had in pasting up the front of the Union League Club.

The week before April first we chartered a Chinatown bus and drove down to Washington stopping at Jersey City, Bayonne, Newark, Elizabeth, Philadelphia, Baltimore, and many other cities and towns on the way, holding street meetings and sometimes meetings in rented halls. By that time the war spirit had become so feverish that our meetings were broken up as fast as we started them. Then we had to climb back into the bus and speed on to the next stopping place where we would make another attempt. There was a riot in Baltimore. We were holding a most dignified meeting in the auditorium when groups of Catholic college students disrupted the meeting. The speakers were booed from the platform and the police broke up the meeting. Out in front of the hall the rioting continued, and standing in the thick of it by one of the police wagons trying to find out whether it was our own or the disrupters who were being arrested, I had two ribs cracked by a policeman's club. I had my newspaper card pinned on my coat, but no credentials were of any account in such a disturbance. The policeman who struck me had blood streaming from his forehead from some missile that was thrown at him and he could scarcely see in the mob that was pressing close around him. Two of our crowd who were arrested were released immediately, and the next morning we proceeded on our way.

A few days after, war was declared, and there was nothing for us to do but go back to New York and work with the Anti-Conscription League. The work that we had to do then was to persuade people not to register for the draft.

Not long after this I left *The Call* and worked for a time with the Anti-Conscription League. I was the only paid member of the group, drawing a salary of fifteen dollars a week. The rest of the crowd were all college students, and they needed someone to keep the office open, answer letters, and handle publicity. I did not stay there very long as the *Masses* offered me a job as assistant editor, and I began the more leisurely life of working for a monthly publication. I continued going around with the Anti-Conscription League members as well as with the Socialists. Jack Reed's and Arturo Giovannitti's poems in the *Masses* stirred the blood, and the one on the murder of Frank Little I can remember to this day. He was one of the Everett I.W.W.'s who was taken out by an armed mob and hanged from a railroad trestle.

There were cartoons and drawings by Art Young, Hugo Gellert, Boardman Robinson, Maurice Becker, and Glintenkamp. Max Eastman carried on a controversy with President Wilson, and the letters they exchanged were printed monthly in the paper. Floyd Dell, the managing editor, wrote articles and book reviews and in his spare time was working on a novel. Max Eastman wrote very beautiful lyric poetry and essays on aesthetics. I believe that these older members of the staff were more artists than propagandists.

I spent a great deal of time with Maurice Becker and Mike Gold. There were many afternoons when we took long walks along the Palisades and over on Staten Island. Hugo Gellert used to draw beautiful pastoral pictures for me which Max Eastman helped himself to very charmingly to decorate his apartment.

Most of the artists and writers lived in real poverty, and when some friends of the magazine offered some of us on the staff an apartment in Greenwich Village for the summer, we very joyfully accepted and lived in bourgeois comfort for the next five months. It was on the top floor of an old building in MacDougall Street over the Province-town Players. I occupied the hall bedroom and Floyd Dell, Merrill Rogers, and David Karb took the rest of the apartment. During those months we had many meetings in the two living rooms of the apartment. I remember one meeting especially, the night before men were required to register for the draft, when Max Eastman, Floyd Dell, Jack Reed, the Boni brothers, Hiram Moderwell, Mike Gold, Harold Stearns, and many others spent the entire night discussing whether they should register the next day and then most of them went out and registered.

A good many of my friends during the next year evaded the draft by going to Mexico. The one true, consistent objector I knew at the time was Hugo Gellert's younger brother who was thrown in the guard house in a camp out on Long Island. Deprived of everything but a shirt and trousers, he was put on bread and water. Hugo and I used to go to see him and bring him bars of chocolate and fruit and whatever we could smuggle in. The guards were friendly and permitted us to give him the food. I don't remember what month it was, but the nights were chilly, and one of the guards used to give him a trench coat to cover himself with as he slept on the floor. He had a violin which they smuggled in to him so that he could sit and play to wile away not only his long hours but those of the guards. And then suddenly we heard that he had committed suicide the day after we had visited him. We had left him laughing and cheerful. He had been murdered, Hugo insisted, convinced that his brother was not the one to seek death as a way out, coming as he did from a family of Hungarian revolutionists.

During the course of the summer Max Eastman went on a speaking trip to raise funds for the *Masses,* and Floyd Dell left for a month's vacation. I had the job of selecting material, making up the paper that month, and it was some of the articles and cartoons in that issue that led to the indictment of the editors on the charge of treason. Suppression had been threatened for the past few months, and it was only a matter of time before the paper had to cease publication, so no one felt that I had precipitated matters. The trials did not take place until the following winter.

During that summer Rayna came to visit me from Chicago, and we spent many a night roaming the streets with Mike, Maurice, Hugo, and others, ending up at the apartment for coffee and discussion. We used to pick up people we encountered in the parks and bring them home with us. Sentimental charity some of the others called it. Mike Gold recognized it as an expression of what he called my religious instinct. We were both reading Tolstoi at the time and were thoroughly in sympathy with the Christianity he expressed, the Christianity that dispensed with a church and a priesthood.

In the fall, after Rayna had gone home, I went down to Washington with the League for the Defense of Political Prisoners to picket the White House, which had been besieged by suffragists for some months. A large number of the suffragists had been in jail, sometimes as many as twenty-five at a time, many for as long as sixty days, sentences which they served in the workhouse at Occoquan.

Two of the leaders were hunger striking, demanding the right to be treated as political prisoners instead of being forced to work, wear prison clothing, and be deprived of books and mail. The rights of political prisoners were recognized by most European countries, even by Russia under the czars. As a matter of fact, most of the revolutionists who spent long terms in jail and had been in exile in Siberia had used the opportunity given them by the government to study Marxism, and history in the light of Marxism, solidifying their influence as intellectual leaders of the masses.

But in Washington the suffragists were treated as criminals and shared cells with petty thieves and prostitutes. The suffragists had recruited a large number of women from all over the United States, reflecting all classes of society, to picket with them in protest against the brutal treatment they had received. The wife of the president of the Board of Trustees of Bellevue Hospital was among them. There were society women from Boston and Philadelphia, one dignified old lady from Florida, school girls, and teachers.

We all met at headquarters and started our slow march in front of the gates of the White House. Usually the police gathered up the pickets as fast as they appeared, but on these days that we picketed, there were small riots and on the first day some of the United States Marines tore our banners from our hands and destroyed them. Those banners that we were able to save were loaded into the police wagons with us, and we made a gay sight through the streets of Washington with the placards hanging out of the back of the police truck. The first day we were discharged on bail. After the second picketing the women refused to give bail and were held over night at the detention house in Washington where army cots had to be set up to hold so large a crowd. The next day all of us were sentenced to thirty days and taken down to the workhouse at Occoquan.

We went by train escorted by many guards. It was fall and the countryside was beautiful in the dusk. It was pitch dark when we reached the workhouse and were forced by the guards to the superintendent's receiving office. They went out of their way to be rough, pulling us by our arms over the country road through the dark, and practically throwing us into the room. After they had taken away our belongings we were all assigned to cells, and those of us who had been vigorous in protest at the rough treatment were assigned to a punishment block of cells where usually prisoners were kept in solitary confinement. There was only a single bunk in each cell, but there were so many of us that they put two in each one, and I shared that of Lucy Burns, a red-headed school teacher from Brooklyn who was one of the leaders of the suffragists.

I had tried to get up in the reception hall of the punishment cell block to join a young artist whom I knew on the other side of the room, and as I moved, four guards jumped upon me as though they were indulging in a football game and I were the football. Other women arose to my assistance, and immediately there was a mad scuffle, a most disgraceful scene where dignified women tore at the guards, bit and kicked and were belabored in turn.

When Lucy Burns was flung into the cell with me she stood by the barred door and began calling to some of the other women to see if they had been injured. She refused to heed the orders of the superintendent to "shut up" and he came to the cell, his face livid with rage, and ordered the guards to handcuff her to the bars. She was forced to stand there for several hours with her arms up above her head. Later on when they released her they left the handcuffs on all night, and the two of us, on the single bunk that had neither mattress, blankets, nor sheets, lay there in our clothes and talked through a good part of the night. I remember we talked about all the novels of Joseph Conrad that we had read. Her favorite was a story called *Youth*.

All of us went on a hunger strike immediately. On the second day we were really put into solitary. The hours were interminably long. I lay there on my bunk watching the slit in the upper part of the cell through which thin sunlight streamed part of the day. I could hear birds outside and the sound of the guards walking in the corridors. But otherwise there was complete silence. The barred door opened on a corridor and every now and then a guard came and looked in. There was a toilet in one corner of the cell which had to be flushed from outside of the cell. We were supposed to call the guard for this attention. Once a day one of the guards would escort us to a wash room at the end of the building. We went one by one, and only encountered our fellow prisoners on these occasions. There was no chance to exchange a word.

The first day our clothes had been taken away from us and we had been presented with prison garments — Mother Hubbard dresses, chemises made of coarse, unbleached muslin and two shoes which were exactly alike.

After the first few days, I asked one of the guards for a Bible as I knew it would be the only thing allowed, and I lay there reading the Psalms by the hour.

Going without food was not hard at all. We drank plenty of water and there was nothing to do. There were so many of us that they could not forcibly feed us all. That torture they saved for the leaders of the group. Thank God I wasn't a leader! The woman in the next cell was forcibly fed and I could hear her struggles as the four guards held her down on the bed and the doctor and his assistant forced a tube down her throat through which they poured beaten egg and milk.

Altogether we were on hunger strike for ten days, and this was most effective. It aroused the protest of the nation. At the end of ten days our demand to be treated as political prisoners was granted. Naturally, we were not forced to work while we were on hunger strike, and when the strike was ended, our own clothes and books were given back to us and we were permitted to receive mail. From then on we were treated with great tenderness when it came to food. They broke our fast with milk toast, and after a day of that we had a most delicious chicken dinner.

That same day we were transferred to the Washington city jail. All of us were taken in cars back to Washington. The beautiful fall weather was invigorating, and we all felt triumphant at the success of the strike. There had been real suffering and misery in the workhouse but from now on imprisonment was more or less of a lark. We were assigned to cells in the Washington jail, and the doors were left unlocked all the time so that we could roam through the prison corridors and visit back and forth and buy food and cigarettes and in general entertain ourselves. There was a phonograph and in the early evening there even was dancing. I remember one afternoon lying in my bunk with a large dish of baked beans, baked by the Negro cook, which were good as candy, sweetened as they were with molasses. I had a book to read, *Fortitude* by Hugh Walpole, while Peggy, my roommate, sat in her lower bunk drawing sketches of the other prisoners.

At the end of sixteen days President Wilson signed a pardon for us all, and we were released. Those last few days, aside from the fact that we were prisoners, were nothing, but the first six days of imprisonment were miserable. In spite of the fact that I was with scores of other women I felt a sense of complete solitude lying behind the bars. I felt keenly the misery of all those others in jail for criminal offenses. My own sentence of thirty days seemed interminable and when I thought of long sentences and even six months seemed terribly long, I was overcome by the misery of those about me. The cause for which we were in jail seemed utterly unimportant. I had not much interest in the vote, and it seemed to me our protest should have been not for ourselves but for all those thousands of prisoners throughout the country, victims of a materialistic system. They were enduring punishment which would not cure them nor deter them from future crimes, and they were being punished by men not much better than themselves, indeed, far worse in some cases.

The one thing our combined protest did affect was the removal of the superintendent, Whittacker, from his position at the workhouse. Our testimony and the affidavits we were able to collect as to his brutality were sufficient.

I truly suffered that first week and the reading of the Bible intensified that suffering. I felt that we were a people fallen from grace and abandoned by God. I felt that we were indeed children of wrath and that a personal conversion was necessary before any revolution could be successful. At the same time I felt that my attitude was morbid. I distrusted my own emotions, feeling that they arose from my long fast and the imprisonment, and besides I felt a sense of shame in turning to God in despair. There was in my heart that insinuation of my college professor that religion was for the weak and those who needed solace and comfort, who could not suffer alone but must turn to God for comfort—to a God whom they themselves conjured up to protect them against fear and solitude.

After I came back from Washington, I freelanced for a while, living in one furnished room after another, moving from the lower East Side to the upper East Side and then again down to the lower West Side of town. It was a bitterly cold winter and the rooms I lived in were never really heated. There was a coal shortage that winter and heatless Mondays were instituted. Usually it was pleasanter to stay out of my room, so there was a great deal of visiting of friends, of hanging around the Provincetown Players where a few of my friends had plays in rehearsal. In the evening the usual meeting place was the back room of an old saloon on the corner of Fourth Street and Sixth Avenue.

Soon I began work on *The Liberator,* a successor to the *Masses,* edited by Crystal Eastman, Max's sister, Eugene O'Neill, Terry Karlin, an old Irishman who knew the Haymarket martyrs in Chicago, Hypolyte Havel, the editor of an anarchist publication, who had been in jails all over Europe for his convictions, Michael Gold and others, were my constant companions on these long evenings. No one ever wanted to go to bed, no one ever wanted to be alone.

It was on one of these cold, bitter winter evenings that I first heard *The Hound of Heaven,* that magnificent poem of Francis Thompson. Gene could recite all of it, and he used to sit there, looking dour and black, his head sunk on his chest, sighing, "And now my heart is as a broken fount wherein tear-drippings stagnate." It is one of those poems that awakens the soul, recalls to it the fact that God is its destiny. The idea of this pursuit fascinated me, the inevitableness of it, the recurrence of it, made me feel that inevitably I would have to pause in the mad rush of living to remember my first beginning and last end.

Mike Gold and Tolstoi, whose books we read, had recalled me to a remembrance of spiritual things the summer before, and now it was Eugene O'Neill and *The Hound of Heaven*. Neither of them knew perhaps how profoundly moved I was. I did my best to hide it, but I was again "tormented by God."

You will be surprised but there was many a morning after sitting all night in taverns or coming from balls over at Webster Hall that I went to an early Mass at St. Joseph's Church on Sixth Avenue. It was just around the corner from where I lived, and seeing people going to an early weekday Mass attracted me. What were they finding there? I seemed to feel the faith of those about me and I longed for their faith. My own life was sordid and yet I had had occasional glimpses of the true and the beautiful. So I used to go in and kneel in a back pew of St. Joseph's, and perhaps I asked even then, "God, be merciful to me, a sinner."

The trial of the editors of the *Masses* came up that winter and I was subpoenaed as a witness for the state. Morris Hillquit, the Socialist attorney, whom I admired as a scholar and a gentleman, defended them and we worked together over the testimony. I was a very bad witness for the state and a very good one for the defense.

Then suddenly a succession of incidents and the tragic aspect of life in general began to overwhelm me and I could no longer endure the life I was leading. Some friends of my family were nurses and it was war time and though

I was still bitterly pacifist, I decided nursing the sick was not contrary to my beliefs by any means. So many nurses had joined the Red Cross and had gone abroad that there was a great need for nurses at home. By January 1, 1918, I had signed up as a probationer in Kings County Hospital in Brooklyn.

Chapter Eight

THE RIGOROUS LIFE

FROM THE BEGINNING I loved the work. I had been used to a great deal of physical activity, both at home and in school. I had been used to a good deal of manual labor, work that was hard and rigorous and which for that very reason made mental activities the more stimulating. Reporting on *The Call* and the daily "foot" work covering assignments kept me healthy. Life among the liberals and the artists I both enjoyed and despised. I was trying to write but my life was undisciplined. I longed for the rigor of those earlier years. I was just as much interested in the labor movement, but it was myself that I felt to be out of tune.

Writing alone did not satisfy me, and the labor movement went dead on me for that time. Workers were getting higher wages than ever before and were not interested in building up an industrial democracy. It was the heyday of the American Federation of Labor. Nobody cared that the great mass of workers was unorganized. A great number of Socialists throughout the country had thrown themselves into the war to end wars, "to make the world safe for democracy." I saw another slogan recently which they will probably use in the next war, admirably vague, "to save humanity from itself."

The A.F. of L. endorsed the war and was just as loud in its condemnation of those who continued to protest it. But it was not the radical movement which I felt had failed me. There were still such men as Debs, whose Canton speech will resound forever in the ears of the workers. On June 16, 1918, he made his famous speech and was sentenced to ten years for his anti-war stand. He said to the court before sentence was passed on him:

Your honor, years ago I recognized my kinship with all living beings, and I made up my mind that I was not one whit better than the meanest on earth. I saw then, and I say now, that while there is a lower class, I am in it, while there is a criminal element I am of it, and while there is a soul in prison I am not free. I listened to all that was said in this court in support and justification of this prosecution but my mind remains unchanged. I look upon the Espionage law as a despotic enactment in flagrant conflict with democratic principles and with the spirit of free institutions. Your honor, I have stated in this court that I am opposed to the social system in which we live; that I believe in a fundamental change — but if possible by peaceable and orderly means. I am thinking this morning of the men in the mills and factories; of the men in the mines and on the railroads. I am thinking of the women who for a paltry wage are compelled to work out their barren lives; of the little children who in this system are robbed of their childhood and in their tender years are seized in the remorseless grasp of Mammon and forced into the industrial dungeons, there to feed the monster machines while they themselves are being starved and stunted, body and soul. I see them dwarfed and diseased and their little lives broken and blasted because in this high noon of our twentieth century Christian civilization money is still much more important than the flesh and blood of childhood. In very truth gold is god today and rules with pitiless sway in the affairs of men.

In this country, the most favored beneath the bending skies, we have vast areas of the richest and most fertile soil, material resources in inexhaustible abundance, the most marvelous productive machinery on earth, and millions of eager workers ready to apply their labor to that machinery to produce in abundance for every man, woman, and child and if there are still vast numbers of our people who are the victims of poverty and whose lives are an unceasing struggle all the way from youth to old age, until at last death comes to their rescue and stills their aching hearts and lulls these hapless victims to dreamless sleep, it is not the fault of the Almighty; it cannot be charged to nature, but it is due entirely to the outgrown social system in which we live that ought to be abolished not only in the interest of the toiling masses but in the higher interest of all humanity.

It was my great good fortune, one month after I began training in the hospital, that a Miss Adams entered and was given the room next to mine. She and I were the newest probationers so we worked together. She was almost thirty years old and had had to delay entering on account of the illness of her father and other family obligations. She was almost the oldest of the nurses in training and the fact that her vocation, as you might call it, had been delayed for so many years made her throw herself into the work with all the more intensity.

All that was necessary to enter training at that time was two years of high school. We supplied our own uniforms and textbooks for the first three months, but after that the hospital supplied both and paid us ten dollars a month. There were not more than a dozen probationers and since the training was severe quite a few dropped out. The work was hard, but Miss Adams brought to it a joy and enthusiasm that was contagious. She was a Catholic, and I was in such close association with her for the coming year that I came to admire her greatly and to associate all her natural goodness and ability with her Catholicism. She didn't go to Mass more than once a week, she never spoke of her faith. She had no Catholic literature in her room aside from her

96

prayer book, and she didn't use that except on special occasions. She was the average kind of Catholic whose faith was so solid a part of her life that she didn't need to talk about it. I felt the healthiness of her soul. I felt that it was strong and vigorous, but she did not discuss it any more than she would discuss the health of her body. I began to go to Mass with her on Sunday mornings even though it meant going without a few hours of much needed sleep. Mass was at five o'clock or five-thirty, and we worked from seven to seven with half a day off on Sunday and half a day during the week. We were supposed to have two hours off in the afternoon, but during those two hours there were classes.

Since so many nurses had enlisted for the Red Cross, often there was no more than one nurse to fifty patients. Even though we were probationers and not given very much responsibility, and there were ward maids and orderlies to take care of many of the disagreeable details, we had a great deal of physical labor. It was a city hospital and patients had to be very sick before they were admitted. We had to change each bed every day, bathe all our patients, rub them down with alcohol, dress bed sores, give out the medicines, attend demonstrations, and generally assist in the irrigations and injections, tappings for spinal and lung fluid, and all the other treatments for patients in the medical and receiving wards. I had my complete medical training during that year, but I had no experience on the surgical wards except a few months with fracture and tonsil cases.

My work was made happier by the companionship of Miss Adams. Sometimes we were on the same ward together or had adjoining wards. That was the year of the influenza epidemic, and we worked so hard that we fell unconscious into our beds at night and had to drag ourselves out of sleep in the morning. I had to take cold baths when I got up because if I got into warm water I fell asleep. Most of the nurses were keen and zealous over the work. We were all so busy we did not have time to suffer over the human misery we saw, although it was heartbreaking to see young people dying all around us of the flu. Often we had to prepare for the morgue as many as eight corpses a day.

Every morning we were expected to have our wards in order by ten o'clock, and it used to give me pleasure to see everyone cleaned and washed and neatly tucked under white counterpanes in the long rows. They were good patients because they were poor and did not expect too much. They were uncomplaining, and they accepted their suffering with stoicism. They did get good food and clean bedding. In the middle of the morning we gave everyone eggnogs, and in the male wards most of the men who were in the habit of drinking got a good stiff drink of whiskey in the eggnog. When they were well enough they used to help us in every way they could.

I liked the order of the life and the discipline. By contrast the life that I had been leading seemed disorderly and futile. I thought of the hours it took most women to do their housework and keep their children in order and wondered why our schools did not have courses in homemaking to make people more efficient in this regard. One of the things that this year in the hospital made me realize was that one of the hardest things in the world is to organize ourselves and discipline ourselves. If there was a bell that rang at six o'clock, if there was a program for the day laid out and one were forced by community discipline, one's life fell into efficient, orderly lines. One could accomplish not only what work was laid out but more besides. One got into the habit, in the hospital, of consistent, sustained effort and of disregarding fatigue, both physical and mental.

Before the year was up I took to writing again in brief half hours in the early morning and in the evening. Then I became restless and began rushing over to New York on my half days off looking for intellectual stimulus. After all, I felt that nursing was not my vocation and that my real work was writing and propaganda. By November the war was over. I was working hard all Armistice Day and the constant shriek of factory whistles meant only that patients were being disturbed by the noisy exuberance of the outside world. A terrible wreck on the elevated lines, a gruesome airplane catastrophe in which all were killed, a man dying in the ward — these things had more reality for me than the ending of the war and the signing of the armistice. I would only see life in the things that were immediately about me so that it wasn't my craving to get back into active work in the radical movement, but my own immediate desire to write that led me to give up my work in the hospital.

Chapter Nine

CHICAGO

THE YEARS FROM 1919 to 1921 were given to writing, newspaper work, attendance at meetings, jobs of various kinds in both New York and Chicago. Often there were long periods when I thought only in terms of my own writing, and after days of work I spent the evening hours writing short stories and sketches and plays that were never published. Since I spent my time with artists and writers and those whom radicals termed bourgeois intellectuals, I was not, strictly speaking, close to the radical movement. There has always been that separation between the liberals and radicals, recognized by the Marxists, both Socialists and Communists.

During these years of my early twenties I was in reality living for myself, and personalities rather than ideas influenced me and kept drawing me back to the labor movement. I held many jobs, reporting jobs, covering the courts in Chicago for capitalistic rather than labor papers, proofreading, library work, cashiering in a restaurant, even clerking in Montgomery Ward's where I had to punch a time clock.

101

I spent a year in Europe but because I was associating at that time only with liberals I had no vital contact with what was going on in those countries. My time in England, France, and Italy was spent with people who were only interested in art and literature and were not in any sense propagandists.

I came back from Europe and went back to Chicago where the Communist Party was leading a precarious existence underground. That was the time when meetings were held in the Michigan woods, when there were hundreds arrested, when workers did not know whether they were Socialists, anarchists, I.W.W.'s or whether they were going into the newly forming party. The Socialists were too dull. They had too little vitality as far as I was concerned, and my allegiance for the most part was with the I.W.W.'s whose ideas in regard to solidarity and direct action appealed greatly to my youth.

It was about this time that I had my second jail experience. It came about in a rather peculiar way with none of the respectable circumstances attendant on it as in the Washington experience. I was associated at that time with some I.W.W.'s who had their headquarters on West Madison Street, Chicago. Across the street from their printing office was an old rooming house where a great many of them stayed, and where in true Wobbly fashion they had an everlasting pot of Mulligan on the fire. Everyone who came in was supposed to contribute to the pot whether it were a bunch of carrots, a piece of meat, or a few pounds of potatoes. It was kept going from week to week, and when the funds were low the boys used to beg from grocers in the neighborhood. Those who had funds took care of their companions who had none, and there was a good spirit of comradeship. Their slogan was "An injury to one is an injury to all" and their sense of solidarity went even into housekeeping details.

One of the girls I met had grown up in reformatories and had been a companion of criminals. She had been a pickpocket and shoplifter and had served many terms in jail. At one time in her life she had taken drugs, but she had cured herself of that habit. She was, at this time, unhappily in love with a newspaper man.

One day I opened the paper to find she had taken bichloride of mercury and was in the city hospital. They managed to save her life but when she was released from the hospital she went straight to the I.W.W. lodging house where she knew she would be taken in. I went over to see her in the evening to bring her food and planned to stay for the night with her. She was still ill and very much depressed and not altogether happy that they had dragged her back from death.

We were undressed and getting into bed when a knock came at the door and four men burst in telling us that we were under arrest for being inmates of a disorderly house. Being arrested on the streets of Washington and being arrested when one was lying in bed in a Chicago West Side rooming house are two entirely different things. I had the moral support in the first case of sixty or seventy women who were arrested with me, and it was some technical charge such as obstructing traffic that was made against us. Now we were alone. It made no difference that radical headquarters all over Chicago were being raided and wholesale arrests being made. We could not feel that we were a part of a movement that was suffering persecution. Perhaps we were not sufficiently indoctrinated.

It had not occurred to us that it was unconventional or unseemly to be staying in a lodging house on West Madison Street. As a matter of fact, it was an unfortunate accident that there were only men in the house at that time as both men and women and married couples had stayed there. The ugly fact remained that we were two young girls arrested by four plain-clothes men who refused to leave the room while we got up and dressed for fear we would try to get away by the fire-escape. These were the days of the Palmer red raids when no one was safe. Those were times of persecution for all radicals. However, it is well to remember that now in these years the same things are occurring. At a strike of the Commodore Hotel workers a few years ago the group of girls who were arrested were charged with disorderly conduct and kept in detention cells. The workers who were wounded last year in the Republic Steel riot were arrested on their hospital beds.

After being taken out of the house in company with a few of the men and being forced to stand on the corner with the police while they called the police wagon, we were taken to the West Chicago Avenue Police Station. Most of the men had dived through windows and down fire-escapes and had gotten away. They were wiser than we were, realizing that places where radicals congregated were always liable to this kind of attack. It was just a case of our knowing that these things were occurring every day and yet not realizing that they could occur to us. We were booked on the charge of being inmates of a disorderly house. We were not allowed to use the telephone to get in touch with a lawyer or our friends, although according to law we should have had this privilege.

We were thrown into a large cell that had six beds in it, one of which had been turned upside down by a drunken woman prisoner who had been in it before us. There were no sheets or pillows on the beds, just dirty mattresses. It was midsummer so we had only our dresses to spread over us for sheets. We took off our shoes and stockings and dresses and lay down again to try to sleep. We felt peculiarly exposed and naked lying there in our slips with the open bars of the cell in front of us, opening out into the reception room where the police and plain-clothes men continued to come in all night bringing other prisoners. At the time that the raid was made on the West Madison Street rooming house there were raids made on *bona fide* houses in the Chicago red light district. All during the night women continued to be put in our cell until pretty soon there were about twenty. There were only six single beds. To keep their clothes from being wrinkled the girls took off not only their dresses but their slips. They treated the affair casually as incidental to their profession. Half dressed as they were, they kept running to the bars of the cell.

I felt at first a peculiar sense of disgust and shame at the position I was in, shame because I had been treated as a criminal and made to feel exactly as though I were guilty of the charge on which I had been arrested. But it was only what I could expect, I thought to myself bitterly, under the present social system, and I thought again of Debs' words: "While there is a lower class, I am of it, and while there is a criminal element, I am of it, and while there is a soul in prison, I am not free."

After my first stunned amazement at what had happened, I could lie on the edge of the cot and observe my companions. They seemed to me to be like any other group of working girls, these young women, who had turned to this hideous way of earning a living. Two of them had been picked up on the street and all the rest of them had been taken from the same house. Several of them had children whom they were supporting in schools or boarding houses out of town. I felt peculiarly helpless at not being able to make a telephone call. It was impossible to get in touch with people on the outside and I felt more actually a prisoner than in those six days of solitary confinement at Occoquan. We were there all that night, all the next day, and the next night.

No food was served to us. We were expected to buy it from the jail matron. A sandwich and a cup of coffee cost a dollar. A package of cigarettes or a pack of cards also came to a dollar. If it had not been for our fellow prisoners we would have gone hungry. I had only two dollars with me and Anne, my companion, had nothing. Our fellow prisoners shared their sandwiches with us and kept us supplied with coffee.

Because I was morose and silent, one of them, who had been booked as the keeper of the house, although she was probably not more than twenty-five herself, insisted on trying to comfort me for what she took to be my first experience. "There always has to be a first time," she told me, and she pointed out one of her own girls who was taking it hard.

During that long interminable day three lost children were brought in, and the whole jail was so full that the matron put the children in with us. The girls, who had no sense of modesty before the police or each other, very considerately put on their dresses while the children were with us and one of them sat with a little boy in her arms and rocked him to sleep, keeping the others quiet while she did so. There was one little girl who was brought in late that night who had been found in a doorway claiming she was lost. But it turned out that she was really afraid to go home because she had bought a pocket book with the money her aunt had given her to buy groceries — a piece of childish recklessness for which she was paying dearly. The girls induced her to tell her name and where she lived so that the police could notify her people. Then one of them filled her new pocket book with a clean handkerchief, some rouge and lipstick and powder, the money which she had spent, and gave the aunt a long lecture on the gentleness with which she should treat the little thief. "Punishing her won't do any good," she kept saying. "You've got to be kind to kids. You've got to love them. That's the only way to do anything with them." But the girls could be horribly crude and coarse too.

Before I had merely read about prison life and had agreed with Tolstoi that such punishment of criminals was futile when we were guilty for permitting such a system as ours to exist and that we, too, should bear the penalty for the crimes committed by those unfortunate ones. We all formed part of one body, a social body, and how could any limb of that body commit a crime alone?

We were photographed and finger-printed and finally taken to the morals court. Before we were placed in the detention pen we were examined for venereal diseases. When men are arrested during a Red raid the police can express their brutality with rubber hoses and blackjacks. They can show their scorn and contempt for those who are trying to "undermine" our present system by kicking and beating them until their victims are a degraded mass of quivering flesh. They show more gallantry in regard to the women. They have a more subtle way of affronting their sensibilities. They can charge them with being prostitutes, make them submit to degrading physical examinations, and throw them into the company of those whom they feel should degrade them. But I felt more horror of the police and that police matron during this experience than I did of the women. The women did not disgust me, it was their profession that disgusted me. They themselves may have been superior, as human beings go, to their captors. There was no pride or hypocrisy among them.

Fortunately, in the courtroom where we were brought before the judge, who, of course, was convinced of our guilt and made us feel it, I met a reporter whom I knew. The girls had offered us their own lawyers and offered to see to it that we got bail. It was not without gratitude that I refused this help. I felt I could not use the cheaper methods of the law to extricate myself and yet in the long run it didn't make any difference. My newspaper friend had to see a judge whom he knew to sign a release for us, so I still felt angry for having to get myself out in this way. I would have preferred to spend the ten days at Lawndale Hospital and take any sentence they chose to inflict. What right did I have to avail myself of the friendship of those in power?

There was still another day in jail before we could get out as it was Saturday and the judge was out playing golf. The girls with whom we had spent the last few days in jail tried to leave us some money as they departed gaily, and it was hard not to offend them by refusing. We assured them that we would be out almost immediately. For a few hours we had to sit in the detention pen until all of the prisoners, male and female, had appeared before the judge.

We had the choice of going either to Lawndale Hospital where women prisoners were sent for ten days, as though they were in quarantine, or to the county jail. When they finally took us out to the police wagon in company with some men prisoners who were handcuffed and bloody, I encountered a Communist friend in front of the county building. He was horrified to see me being put into the police wagon, and he spent the rest of the day trying to start the machinery to get me out.

We were taken out to the county jail and were once more stripped and examined by the police matron. Then we were given prison clothes and cells which formed a block around a central recreation room. The windows of the cells themselves opened on the street, and one could look out the window and greet friends below in the street. I had often noticed that sad block and on one occasion I saw a woman standing on the curb with tears running down her face waving to a man in a cell two flights up.

The woman in the cell next to mine was a drug addict who screamed and howled all that long summer afternoon begging to be put out of her misery. She kept beating her head against the cell wall until they had to put her in a straight jacket, but no attempt was made to give her medical treatment.

The system there was to alternate two hours of confinement with two hours of freedom in the recreation hall and the women sat around reading and playing cards and making themselves tea on a little gas burner which was provided, using their own supplies to supplement the early evening meal. By this time the drug addict had quieted herself sufficiently to come out for supper. Although she was a nervous, quivering wretch when they released her, within fifteen minutes after her door was unlocked she had become perfectly normal. My companion Anne pointed out that there were always drugs among the prisoners and that someone had taken pity on her and given her some.

Finally word came to us that we were released, and the prison matron returned our clothes and we went out in the streets free once more. We felt that for years we had been separated from normal, human intercourse and that ages had elapsed since our arrest a few nights before. The efforts of my radical friend, I found out later, had been useless. It was the kind offices of the newspaper man whom I knew which had effected our release.

For a while in Chicago I worked with Robert Minor on the *Liberator.* Minor was a former I.W.W. who had become converted to the Communist cause after a long summer of reading and research. His former wife told me it had been a hard experience for him, making up his mind to leave one organization to which he had pledged his allegiance and enter another. It is difficult for outsiders to realize the bitterness with which Trotskyites, Communists, Socialists, I.W.W.'s, and Anarchists regard each other. Their animosity toward their fellow radicals is often more extreme than that toward those whom they consider the bourgeois and the capitalist classes. Lenin, in advocating a popular front, had often warned against this bitterness, pointing out that as long as the different groups recognized their fundamental philosophical disagreements, they should strive to work together toward immediate social aims in order to win the masses.

I had first heard of Bob Minor when he was working on the Mooney case in California. He had long been a popular cartoonist whose work was well paid for by the capitalist papers. He had sacrificed a good living and his own personal comfort for the cause of the worker. When I had been on the old *Masses,* Max Eastman used to write to him again and again begging for cartoons, but he gave up all his own work in trying to fight the frame-up against Mooney.

My sister was staying with me at that time in Chicago and in midwinter we decided for personal reasons to go down to New Orleans and work there for the winter. We lived on St. Peter Street across the street from the Cabildo and the Cathedral. I found work on a morning newspaper, *The Item,* and that winter I was occupied in straight newspaper work, writing interviews and feature stories. Many evenings I had assignments, but when there were none, and I heard the Cathedral bells ringing for evening devotions, I used to go to church. It was the first time I had been present at Benediction and it made a profound impression on me. The very physical attitude of devotion of those about me made me bow my head. But did I feel the

Presence there? I do not know. But I remembered those lines from the *Imitation:*

> Who, humbly approaching to the fountain of sweetness, doth not carry thence some little sweetness?

> Who, standing by a copious fire, doth not derive therefrom some little heat? (Book 4, Chapter 4)

I wanted to know what the Benediction hymns were and I bought a little manual of prayers at a religious goods store down the street. I read the Mass. I had to be at the office by seven in the morning and Sunday mornings I was too lazy to get up. But I learned a great deal from that little book. I did not know a single Catholic in New Orleans. If any of my associates were nominally Catholic, they did not let me know of it. There was no one for me to talk to. But my devotion was sincere and I continued to make "visits."

Another girl, who is now secretary of the Communist affiliate, the League for Spanish Democracy in Chicago, was living with my sister and me. That Christmas she goodheartedly gave me a rosary for a present and I learned to say it at the evening services in the Cathedral. She was a Russian Jew and did not understand my interest in Catholicism. She just wanted to give me something she thought I'd like. I have not seen this friend since that winter but I shall always remember her with gratitude and love.

That spring there occurred a reversal in my fortunes which brought about a very deep change in my life. During one of these crowded years I wrote a book, a very bad book, which one of the moving picture companies bought on publication. I haven't the slightest idea why they bought it since they never produced it. It was probably just one of many they extravagantly purchased to keep some other moving picture company from producing it. They paid, to them a very small sum, which to me was the very large sum of five thousand dollars, two thousand of which went to my publishers.

My reaction was that of many other radicals — now I could at last have a home of my own and a quiet spot off in the country where there would be time for study and writing and that small measure of security necessary for that work. Practically all my friends had succumbed to this temptation to private property. Max Eastman and Floyd Dell both had little homes up in Croton, New York. Jack Reed had had a place of his own. Most of the others on the staff of the *Masses* had bought old farms. Mike Gold and Manuel Granich bought a place later, near mine on the beach, and those who could not afford to buy usually rented little places outside of New York or Chicago and spent their summers or week-ends there. Neither New Jersey nor Long Island appealed to me. But I wanted to be by the water, so I bought a small bungalow with a plot of ground twenty by eighty feet on Raritan Bay on Staten Island.

When I was a child, my sister and I used to keep notebooks in the publishers' dummies we occasionally got hold of. Recording happiness made it last longer, we felt, and recording sorrow dramatized it and took away its bitterness; and often we settled some problem which beset us even while we wrote about it.

Those early diaries had been lost long since, some of them destroyed. But when I moved down to the country and some months later entered into a common law marriage, my peace and happiness were such that I once again took to keeping a notebook.

It was a peace, curiously enough, divided against itself. I was happy but my very happiness made me know that there was a greater happiness to be obtained from life than any I had ever known. I began to read and think and ponder, and I notice from my notebooks that it was at this time that I began to pray more earnestly.

Because I feel that this period of my conversion is so joyous and lovely, I wish to write at length, giving the flavor, the atmosphere, the mood of those days.

So I continue from those notebooks that I filled so copiously, especially during the long first winters of the few years I spent in the country.

Chapter Ten

PEACE

October 1925

E VERY YEAR the beaches around New York change, but so gradually, one notices the changes only year by year. The shore line down by our little house is irregular with many little bays and creeks wandering inland every few miles. In addition, small piers and breakwaters have been built which either take away the sand or pile it up. Some years before a pier a quarter of a mile down the beach toward the open ocean fell to ruin in a storm with the result that the sand is washed away from our beach to be piled up on the next one.

This leaves a big expanse of rocky wasteland, varied in color and mottled with green and red seaweed. It is a paradise for children, though hard on their bare feet. They grow accustomed to it, however, and can soon walk lightly among the stones, finding all kinds of crabs and little fish and eels caught in the pools at low tide. Every now and then I can find a lobster or blue shell crab, or a big eel; and of course there are killies, snails, and hermit crabs. We are always making collections of them.

Bait diggers come from miles around, old, gaunt, and weatherbeaten, most of them bending for hours over their digging forks, getting foot-long sand-worms and blood-worms which they sell for fifty cents a dozen. These quiet old men bring their lunches with them and seek out a sheltered spot at noon where they can eat and rest. I go down to the bait diggers and pick up the clams as they turn them up in their search for worms.

The seagulls scream over the rocks, blue and gray and dazzling white, winging their way from the wreck of the old excursion boat to the larger rocks in the water, diving with a splash into the shallow gray water for a fish. The waves, the gulls, and the cawing of the crows in the woods in back of the house are the only sounds on these fall days.

On calm days the waves come gliding in, laughing, gurgling, chasing, and overtopping each other, hastening sideways, crablike, breaking at one end into a plumy white crest which slides quickly through the wave until it crashes against the shingle on the beach.

Farther up and down the beach, away from our tiny bay, the waves roll in from the ocean, crashing dull and ominous on the sands, but there by the house, except during storms, the waves are gentle and playful.

I wander every afternoon up and down the beach for miles, collecting mussels, garlanded in seaweed, torn loose from the piers, pockets full of jingle shells which look as though they are made of mother of pearl and gunmetal.

117

When the tide goes out these little cups of shells are left along the beach, each holding a few drops

The little house I have furnished very simply with a drift-wood stove in one corner, plenty of books, comfortable chairs and couches, and my writing table in the window where I can look out at the water all day. On the walls hang the fruits of my collecting — horseshoe crabs, spider crabs, the shell of a huge sea turtle, whelks' cocoons, hanging like false curls, several mounted fish heads, boards covered with starfish, sea horses, pipe and file fish, all picked up in little pools at low tide.

◆ ◆ ◆

It is an international neighborhood down here near the end of Staten Island. Down the beach are a Belgian couple, next door in an old hotel is an Italian woman from Bleecker Street who takes in boarders during the summer. The grocer and the hardware man are Irish. There are five other bungalows in our small colony, two Catholic families, and a widow of German descent. The other two houses are occupied by my own friends who moved down here after I did, Russian and Rumanian Jews.

Down on the beach in a tiny shack lives a beachcomber and fisherman who is a friend of the entire neighborhood. His home is six by eight feet in size, just big enough for a bed, stove, and chair, and there he lives winter and summer.

"I'm very happy as I am," he says. "Everybody says to me, 'Smiddy, why don't you get to work this winter and do some painting for me.' But what happens when I do get work? Last spring I painted Mr. Cleary's house for him and I kept drinking his liquor that he sells. By the time I got through I didn't have a cent of money coming to me, but he handed me a bill for ten dollars. Money is bad for me. I know it. I can trade my fish and clams for oil and food and what else do I need?" And he waved his arms expansively around and indicated the beauties of his life.

He keeps his shack in good order, with crab traps, clam forks, and fishing paraphernalia suspended from the ceiling.

I sit down on the sand in front of his cabin in a steamer chair which he keeps especially for me, and watch him cook. This afternoon the delicious smell of fried mushrooms perfumed the air. Afternoons we spend in the fields gathering pounds of them. There had been a bitter wind blowing today but we were bundled up and it was fun peering around in the dry grass. At first I could hardly tell them from the many round white pebbles that dotted the sandy soil in the fields.

Smiddy still had lobster pots out and when he pulled them in this morning he found lobsters and a few crabs. In addition to all these delicacies he has a huge frying pan full of potatoes, and another of whiting, which are coming in so thick this fall that we have to carry them in bushel baskets. I am salting them down.

Late this afternoon the wind dropped and the door of Smiddy's shack stood open and he sat there contemplating the sunset. The waves lapped the shore, tingling among the shells and pebbles, and there was an acrid odor of smoke in the air. Down the beach the Belgians were working, loading rock into a small cart which looked like a tumbrel drawn by a bony white horse. They stooped as though in prayer, outlined against the brilliant sky, and as I watched, the bell from the chapel over at St. Joseph's rang the Angelus. I found myself praying, praying with thanksgiving, praying with open eyes, while I watched the workers on the beach, the sunset, and listened to the sound of the waves and the scream of snowy gulls.

"Coffee?" Smiddy asked me, and I accepted the big cup from his hand and bit into a thick slice of buttered toast with fried mushrooms on top.

Later this evening the wind rose again and whistled around the house, and the noise of the sea is loud. I read now evenings until late in the night, and in my preoccupation the fire goes out, so that I have to get into bed to keep warm, clutching my books with ice cold hands.

October 15

Some of Mrs. Mario's boarders are *still* with her, one a mother with several children.

This morning I was standing at the head of the steps leading down to the beach — it was too wet to sit any place, — and leaning against the dead pine tree, I looked out at a four-masted schooner putting up sail. It was peaceful, and there was a heavenly, pearly radiance about the water, the boat, and the sky. It had been raining all night and the waves were high, steadily pouring in, making the sound of a waterfall, a constant rush of water. The tide was out, leaving bare rocks covered with seaweed. The rank smell of the sea was strong and pleasant. But now a child's wails broke the stillness and I saw the Italian mother of four little girls, rushing down the steps to the beach with a stick in her hand. One of the children had just run out of the house and taken refuge on the sand.

I recognized that it was little Dorrie who was crying, and I felt a wave of resentment against the mother and against the three other little girls who were following her excitedly, with the ugly excitement that is strong in many children at the sight of another's suffering.

Why didn't she leave the child alone down there on the breakwater, to get over her grief, anger, or whatever it was? But the child stood there shrieking as she saw her mother coming toward her with a switch, and her cry held a note of bitter unhappiness.

The bright cerise shawl of the rugged Italian woman, striding over the sand, billowed out in back of her with the wind. She switched the child and then strode back up the beach to the summer house where she sat with the other children who had followed her gloating. Every now and then one of the other children ran over to little Dorrie to say something to her but she repulsed them and continued crying.

I felt that I could not stand it and went into the house looking for something to give the child. On one of the bookcases there is a little statuette of the Blessed Virgin that Peggy Baird gave me. It is made of wax and stands under a glass case. A friend of hers, not a Catholic (and neither is Peggy), brought it from Czechoslovakia and I love it dearly. She is dressed in the brightest of blue capes over a white dress with a golden girdle and golden bands around the neck and hem. Her flaxen hair, also made of wax, hangs around her shoulders. There is a garland of roses around her head to which is attached a golden halo which resembles a watch spring pulled out. She stands on a bright blue ball the same color as her cape and around the ball is entwined a snake, bright green with a pink and yellow apple in its red mouth. And the blue ball stands on grass which is like green noodles, garlanded with little rose-buds. It is very sweet but it is very fragile, already cracked down the back of the cape.

I would have liked very much to bring it down to Dorrie to see if it would comfort her but there were too many people around. Mannie and Mike had just come up from the beach and were hanging over the pool in the garden into which they had just put some kitties, a snail or two, and a beautiful hound fish. Nickolai, buttoned up to the chin in a heavy sweater, was trying to make a sand-worm pinch the cat's nose to show what nippers it had. Besides these there were the mother and the three little girls sitting down in front of the hotel. No, altogether too many people around. Besides the child might not want it, or if she did, she might be in a mood to repulse any offers of sympathy.

What if she knocked the statuette out of my hand? I loved it too much myself to risk it. I suddenly felt that it was the most precious possession I had. Besides I'd feel embarrassed if the child repulsed me. With such thoughts are our humane impulses overruled?

So I went back to the kitchen, sighing, looking for a piece of cold toast and cheese, and when I came back, Dorrie had stopped crying, had stopped nursing her sore little legs, and was bending over the aquarium with Nick.

November

Mother sent me some of my high school books (now that I have a place of my own to keep them in) and the other day I came across these words, written on a faded slip of paper in my own writing. I do not remember writing them.

"Life would be utterly unbearable if we thought we were going nowhere, that we had nothing to look forward to. The greatest gift life can offer would be a faith in God and a hereafter. Why don't we have it? Perhaps like all gifts it must be struggled for. 'God, I believe' (or rather, 'I must believe or despair'), 'Help Thou my unbelief.' 'Take away my heart of stone and give me a heart of flesh.' "

"It is interesting to note that these requests are mandatory. It is as though God expected us to demand these things as our right, not to plead for them as favors. 'Give

123

us this day our daily bread,' not 'We beseech Thee to give us.'"

"As to religious exercises, are not all those things silly? Yet to make the body strong there must be physical exercise, discipline, and exertion. Then why not exercises for the soul, to be done whether we care for them or not, automatically if we must, at first, — strainingly, gropingly, if we feel that way about it, but do them we must."

I wrote the above lines when I felt the urgent need for faith, but there were too many people passing through my life, — too many activities, — too much pleasure (not happiness).

I have been passing through some years of fret and strife, beauty and ugliness, days and even weeks of sadness and despair, but seldom has there been the quiet beauty and happiness I have now. I thought all those years I had freedom, but now I feel that I had neither real freedom nor even a sense of freedom.

And now, just as in my childhood, I am enchained, tied to one spot, unable to pick up and travel from one part of the country to another, from one job to another. I am enchained because I am going to have a baby. No matter how much I may wish to flee from my quiet existence sometimes, I cannot, nor will be able to for several years. I have to accept my quiet and stillness, and accepting it, I rejoice in it.

For a long time now, I had thought I could not have a child. A book I read years ago in school, *Silas Marner,* expressed the sorrow of a mother bereft of her child, and it expressed, too, my sorrow at my childless state. Just a few months ago I read it again, with a longing in my heart for a baby. My home, I felt, was not a home without one. The simple joys of the kitchen and garden and beach brought sadness with them because I had not the companionship of a child. No matter how much one is loved or one loves, that love is lonely without a child. It is incomplete.

And now I know that I am going to have a baby.

Still November

I was thinking the other day of how inadequately we pray. Often in saying the Our Father, I find myself saying by rote the first four lines and throwing my heart into the last, asking for bread and grace and forgiveness. This selfishness humiliates me so that I go back to the beginning again in order to give thanks. "Hallowed be Thy Name. Thy kingdom come." Often I say no other prayer.

I am surprised that I am beginning to pray daily. I began because I had to. I just found myself praying. I can't get down on my knees, but I can pray while I am walking. If I get down on my knees I think, "Do I really believe? Whom am I praying to?" And a terrible doubt comes over me, and a sense of shame, and I wonder if I am praying because I am lonely, because I am unhappy.

But when I am walking up to the village for the mail, I find myself praying again, holding the rosary in my pocket that Mary Gordon gave me in New Orleans two years ago.

Maybe I don't say it right but I keep saying it because it makes me happy.

Then I think suddenly, scornfully, "Here you are in a stupor of content. You are biological. Like a cow. Prayer with you is like the opiate of the people." And over and over again in my mind that phrase is repeated jeeringly, "Religion is the opiate of the people."

"But," I reason with myself, "I am praying because I am happy, not because I am unhappy. I did not turn to God in unhappiness, in grief, in despair, — to get consolation, to get something from Him."

And encouraged that I am praying because I want to thank Him, I go on praying. No matter how dull the day, how long the walk seems, if I feel low at the beginning of the walk, the words I have been saying have insinuated themselves into my heart before I have done, so that on the trip back I neither pray nor think but am filled with exultation.

Along the beach I find it appropriate to say the Te Deum which I learned in the Episcopalian church. When I am working about the house, I find myself addressing the Blessed Virgin and turning toward her statue.

It is so hard to say how this delight in prayer has been growing on me. Two years ago, I was saying as I planted seeds in the garden, "I must believe in these seeds, that they fall into the earth and grow into flowers and radishes and beans. It is a miracle to me because I do not understand it. Neither do naturalists understand it. The very fact that

126

they use glib technical phrases does not make it any the less a miracle, and a miracle we all accept. Then why not accept God's miracles?"

I am going to Mass now regularly on Sunday mornings.

November Still

I am alone these days. Fred is in town all week, only coming out weekends and a few nights. I have finished the writing I was doing and feel at a loose end, thinking enviously of my friends going gaily about the city, about their work, with plenty of companionship.

Just because I feel restless, it is a very good reason to stay down here and content myself with my life as a sybaritic anchorite. For how can I be a true anchorite with such luxuries as a baby to look forward to, not to speak of the morning paper, groceries delivered at the door, a beach to walk on, and the water to feast my eyes on? And then the fresh fish and clams, oysters and mushrooms, Jerusalem artichokes, and such delicacies. I shall invite Smiddy up to supper tonight and discuss with him the painting of the room. I shall read Dickens this evening.

◆ ◆ ◆

In spite of my desire for a sociable week in town, in spite of a desire to pick up and flee from my solitude, I take pleasure in thinking of the idiocy of the pleasures I would indulge in if I were there. Teas and dinners, the conversation or lack of it, dancing in a smoky crowded room when one might be walking on the beach, — the dull restless cogitations which come after dissipating one's energies, — these things strike me with renewed force every time I have spent days in the city. My virtuous resolutions to indulge in such pleasure no more are succeeded by a hideous depression when neither my newfound sense of religion, my family life, my work, nor my surroundings seem sufficient to console me. I think of death and am overwhelmed by the terror and the blackness of both life and death. And I long for a church near at hand where I can go and lift up my soul.

When I am feeling these things I cannot write them, and while I am writing them I write almost self-consciously, wondering if I am not exaggerating, but the mood which possessed me yesterday was real enough and during the evening I read desperately, trying to rescue myself from the wall of silence which seemed to close me in.

But this makes me realize that often talk is an escape from doing anything. We chatter on and on to cover our feelings and to hide from ourselves and others our own futility.

Of course conversation is often spirited and uplifts me as some books do. It helps me to glimpse the meaning in things and jolts me out of the rut in which I have been ambling along. I am spurred on to the pursuit of knowledge by a renewed love of knowledge. And yet the trouble with these conversations is that often they are not spontaneous. Some of my liberal friends, for instance, have gatherings,

Sunday afternoons or Thursday nights, and the little crowd which comes feels itself a group and the conversation often seems pompous and self-congratulatory.

This exaltation of the articulate obscures the fact that there are millions of people in this world who feel and in some way carry on courageously even though they cannot talk or reason brilliantly. This very talk may obscure everything that we know nothing of now, and who knows but that silence may lead us to it.

December

It is a sunshiny hazy day and the boats on the bay look ghostlike and unreal. The morning sun makes each blade of grass, each dry twig, stand out and the grasses in the field next to the house do not stir. There are only the starlings to break the silence and occasionally the far-off whistle of the train. Even the waves make no sound upon the beach for there is an offshore wind.

The cats have just been fed a dogfish apiece and are growling at each other under the porch. Fred caught the dogfish last night on the pier and he has been cutting one up to study its insides. No one around here eats them, thinking them not fit for food, except Mrs. Mario who assures us that all Italians think them delicious. So, we shall try them for lunch today.

Did I say the house was silent? Just then there came another sound, loud in the stillness. There is a bucket of soft-shelled clams out in the pantry and they squirt now and then and sound as though they were gasping and sighing.

◆ ◆ ◆

Yesterday was a busy day. We studied biology for an hour or so in the morning in the shape of the larvae of a mussel. We went for a long row along the shore in the afternoon, every now and then stopping to investigate the flotsam and jetsam on the water. Not that the two terms should be used generally. I read a definition of them the other day, according to a Merchant Shipping Act. Flotsam is floating wreck and jetsam is property thrown overboard to avoid wreck, and in early days was distinguished from wreckage cast on the shore by the waves.

It was pleasant rowing about in the calm bay. The oyster boats were all out and far on the horizon, off Sandy Hook, there was a four-masted vessel. I had the curious delusion that several huge holes had been stove in her side, through which you could see the blue sky. The other vessels seemed sailing in the air, quite indifferent to the horizon on which they should properly have been resting. Fred tried to explain to me scientific facts about mirages and atmospheric conditions, and on the other hand, I pointed out to him how our senses lie to us.

But it is impossible to talk to him about religion or faith. A wall immediately separates us. The very love of Nature and study of her secrets which is bringing me to faith, separates him from religion.

Chapter Eleven

NEW LIFE

MY CHILD was born in March at the end of a harsh winter. In December I had to come in from the country and take a little apartment in town. It was good to be there, close to friends, close to a church where I could stop and pray. I read the *Imitation of Christ* a great deal. I knew that I was going to have my child baptized a Catholic, cost what it may. I knew that I was not going to have her floundering through many years as I had done, doubting and hesitating, undisciplined and amoral. I felt it was the greatest thing I could do for a child. For myself, I prayed for the gift of faith. I was sure, yet not sure. I postponed the day of decision.

A woman does not want to be alone at such a time. Even the most hardened, the most irreverent, is awed by the stupendous fact of creation. No matter how cynically or casually the worldly may treat the birth of a child, it remains spiritually and physically a tremendous event. God pity the woman who does not feel the fear, the awe, and the joy of bringing a child into the world.

Becoming a Catholic would mean facing life alone, and I clung to family life. It was hard to contemplate giving up a mate in order that my child and I could become members of the Church. Fred would have nothing to do with religion or with me if I embraced it. So I waited.

Those last months of waiting I was too happy to know the unrest of indecision. I was waiting. The days were slow in passing, but week by week the time came nearer. I spent some time in writing, but in general I felt inactive, incapable of going to meetings, of seeing many people, of taking up the threads of my past life.

And then the little one was born, and with her birth the spring was upon us. My joy was so great that I sat up in bed in the hospital and wrote an article for the *New Masses* about my child, wanting to share my joy with the world. I was glad to write it for a workers' magazine because it was a joy all women know no matter what their grief at poverty, unemployment, and class war.

The article so appealed to my Marxist friends that the account was reprinted all over the world in workers' papers. Diego Rivera, when I met him some four years afterward in Mexico, greeted me as the author of it. And Walt Carmen, who was at that time editor of the *New Masses,* said that it had been printed in Russian newspapers and that I had rubles awaiting me in Moscow.

There was a Catholic girl in the bed next to me in the ward. She was a young Italian, not more than twenty-two, and she had just had her third child. She had a very serious and very obscure heart condition which led every physician who examined her to declare that she should not have children, that death was certain if she did. But she had had three, and, day by day, doctors gathered around her bed to examine her and exclaim over the novelty of her heart disease and expostulate with her for bringing children into the world. Several times they stood there giving her information on birth control and she listened with her eyes cast down, not answering them. They assumed she was stupid and repeated in the simplest phrases their directions, speaking in phrases as they spoke to foreigners who cannot understand English. Then when they looked on her chart and saw she was a Catholic they expressed their impatience and went away.

"I just don't pay any attention," she told me. "God will take care of me. I know I have to be careful. We live on the first floor and I never walk up and down stairs, and my mother-in-law helps me all the time, so I'm all right."

She did not care much for reading, and lay there watching with interested eyes what went on in the ward, that small world in which we were so contentedly confined for ten days.

"What you going to name your baby?" she asked me. "Teresa? I have a medal of the Little Flower here — you can have it if you want it."

I told her I didn't believe in such things, and she didn't take it amiss. "If you like someone, you like to have something to remind you of them," she said, and I was ashamed and took the medal.

Due to an attack of grippe after I left the hospital, Teresa's baptism was postponed for a time. Not being a Catholic myself, and not having been baptized myself until I was twelve, I didn't know the anxiety of Catholic mothers, that feeling almost that the baby had not yet been born until it had been baptized.

When Teresa was six weeks old and I was still very weak, we went down to the country. It was April and though it was still cold, it was definitely spring.

Every morning while Teresa napped on the sunny porch, well swathed in soft woolen blankets, I went down to the beach and with the help of Smiddy brought up driftwood, enough to last until next morning. My husband was home only week-ends and then he chopped enough wood to last a few days. But when the wind was high and piercing it penetrated the house so that much wood was needed, and it was a pleasure to tramp up and down the beach in the bright sun and collect wood which smelled of seaweed, brine, and tar. It was warmer outside than it was in the house, and on the porch Teresa was nicely sheltered. Sometimes in the afternoon I put her in her carriage and went out along the woods, watching, almost feeling the buds bursting through their warm coats. Song sparrows, woodpeckers, hawks, crows, robins, nuthatches, and of course laughing gulls made the air gay with their clamor. Starlings chattered all day in the branches of the old pine in front of the porch. We collected azalea buds, dogwood, sassafras, and apple tree branches to decorate the room. Best of all there were still skunk cabbages small enough to make a most decorative center piece, propped up with stones, gleaming mottled green, dark red and yellow. They were never so colorful as they were that year, and spring after spring since I have watched for them bursting up vigorously in marshy places. Skunk cabbages and the spring peeper mean that the winter is over and gone, and the voice of the swallow is heard in the land.

There was arbutus still buried under the leaves so that you had to look carefully for it like buried treasure. They were spring beauties and adder's tongue and dandelion greens. The year before I had been planting radishes on March first but this year gardening gave way to more delightful tasks.

Supper always was early and the baby comfortably tucked away before it was dark. Then, tired with all the activities that so rejoiced and filled my days, I sat in the dusk in a stupor of contentment. Outside, dozens of fleecy pink clouds were caught in the top of the hickory trees at the bead of the bank and below them were whole fleets of lavender gondolas, then the deeper purple shadows of the Jersey shore. The three lighthouses stood out black against the silver water and there was not a wave, only a rippling, a scalloping along the yellow beach.

Soon the pink and rose clouds faded to a dingy smoke color, and those nearer the horizon changed to a purplish gray. The water remained silver with a peculiar surface glow which the sky did not have though they were the same color. Away off, miles away, through the bare trees on the point, the lights of a roadway flickered like candles.

The meadow before the house became a yellow deeper than the beach with a peculiar afterglow, and at the edge of the meadow, before the bank swept down to the sands, some dead weeds gallantly stood, goldenrod with the tufts still on it, sturdier sumac, and the tangle of wild grape and bayberry bushes. No life was showing on the bare branches of the honey locust trees, those trees so late in budding, but life was there, and life was there too in the room with me, throbbing silently.

And always, those deep moments of happiness gave way to a feeling of struggle, of a long silent fight to be gone through with. There had been the physical struggle, the mortal combat almost of giving birth to a child, and now there was coming the struggle for my own soul. I knew Teresa would be baptized, and I knew also the rending it would cause in human relations around me. I was to be torn and agonized again, I knew, and I was all for putting off the hard day.

Then one afternoon as I wheeled her in her little carriage along the road which led down to St. Joseph's Home, a former estate of Charles Schwab, which had been given to the Sisters of Charity, I met a Sister who was on her way to visit a neighbor of mine.

That estate had been one of my stumbling blocks. I could never pass it without thinking of Schwab's career as head of the Bethlehem Steel Corporation, of his work in breaking the Homestead strike, of how he, to this day, refuses to recognize unions of workers in his Bethlehem Steel Corporation.

I could not but feel that his was tainted money which the Sisters had accepted. It was, I felt, money which belonged to the workers. He had defrauded the worker of a just wage. His sins cried to heaven for vengeance. He had ground the faces of the poor. "Let not the oil of the sinner fatten my head" (Ps. 140:5), I thought with the Psalmist. "He that offereth sacrifice of the goods of the poor, is as one that sacrificeth the son in the presence of his father." "He that sheddeth blood, and he that defraudeth the labourer of his hire, are brothers" (Ecclus. 34:24–27). The words of the son of Sirach went through my brain, wearying me. Yet strangely enough, in bitterness of soul these thoughts led me inevitably to the problem: how to have Teresa baptized.

That bitterness felt by so many in the radical labor movement toward what they call "organized religion" was mixed with the knowledge of the divinity of the Catholic Church. It was ever in my mind that human frailties and the sins and ignorances of those in high places throughout history only proved that the Church *must* be divine to have persisted through the centuries. I would not blame the Church for what I felt were the mistakes of churchmen.

I could only always console myself with Christ's words that the greatest enemies would be those of the "household."

I felt, too, that there were going to be many obstacles put in my path, and that this in a strange way was one of them.

That afternoon I was emboldened by a sense of compulsion to speak to the Sister who was hurrying by me, to ask her how to go about having a baby baptized. I had a warm feeling as I approached her, a feeling that whatever the errors of Charlie Schwab, Sister Aloysia had no part in them in her simplicity and poverty.

She was very matter-of-fact. She seemed to take things for granted, and was not surprised that a mother of a new baby would stop her in this casual fashion and ask her so stupendous a question. Of course a mother, no matter how heathen she might be, would want her baby to be sure of eternal life! She knew of me by reputation — indeed all the neighborhood knew that we and our friends were either Communist or Anarchist in sympathies. But those same dear Catholic neighbors who heard sermons excoriating "the fiendish and foul machinations of the Communists" (I have heard just such expressions used), were kindly people who came to use our telephone and bring us a pie now and then, who played with us on the beach and offered us lifts to the village in their cars. Sister Aloysia, too, had no fear, only a neighborly interest in us all. Perhaps she had been praying for us these past two years as she swept past down

the lane on a visit to some of the Catholics at the end of
the road. Perhaps her work-worn hand was clutching that
rosary which jingled at her side just a little more fervently
and comfortingly.

She felt my liking and I was warmed by her interest.
She took me under her protection immediately. She did
not make little of my difficulties, nor did she think for a
minute that they were insurmountable. There was a hard
row to hoe in front of us, was her attitude, but we could get
through it. She would hang on to that long, formidable-
looking rosary of hers, hang on to it like an anchor, and
together we would ride out the gale of opposition and
controversy. All we had to do was depend on prayer.

And as for practical details, we would just go ahead
as though it were very simple. Did I have any Catholic
relatives?

Yes, there was cousin Grace. She was married and she
and her husband could be reached, though I had not seen
them or any relatives for years.

All right then, she herself, Sister Aloysia, would get in
touch with the parish priest in Tottenville, a young man,
very obliging. He had been coming down to offer up Mass
at the Home and she could see him after breakfast the next
morning.

Somehow or other, with the irregularities of her parents
not being Catholic, Teresa's baptism did not take place until
late June. Sister Aloysia in her anxiety that all should go
well dropped in every day to see if I were persisting in my

determination. She also was quite frank in her anxiety for the baby's welfare. One morning she came rushing up on the porch — "She's not dead yet?" she wanted to know, and then praised God that the baby was living and also struggling toward her baptism. Sister was sure that the powers of darkness were struggling hard for my little one — "He's greedy for souls," she said, meaning the devil, and in this case I had more confidence and hope than she because I assured her Christ must be even more so. Anyway, Teresa thrived lustily and was beginning to throw back her head and crow and gurgle, competing with the birds to make the morning joyful.

"Don't be afraid of this old black crow," Sister used to tell her as she bent over her crib. And Teresa used to open her mouth in a toothless smile, embellished by a delightful dimple which she has since lost.

But Sister Aloysia did not neglect me in her anxiety for the baby. "You must be a Catholic yourself," she kept telling me. She had no reticences. She speculated rather volubly at times on the various reasons why she thought I was holding back. She brought me pious literature to read, saccharine stories of the saints, emasculated lives of saints young and old, back numbers of pious magazines.

William James, agnostic as he was, was more help. He introduced me to St. Teresa of Avila and St. John of the Cross. And I already had St. Augustine and the *Imitation* and the Bible from which I derived strength and comfort.

But isolated as I was in the country, knowing no Catholics except my neighbors who seldom read anything except newspapers and secular magazines, there was not much chance of being introduced to the good literature of the present day. Chesterton's paradoxes wearied me. Belloc's histories I enjoyed but they did not inspire me. I was in a state of dull content — I was not in a state to be mentally stimulated. I was too happy with my child. What faith I had I held on to stubbornly. The need of patience emphasized in the writings of the saints consoled me on the slow road I was traveling. I would put all my affairs in the hands of God and wait.

Three times a week Sister Aloysia came to give me a catechism lesson which I dutifully tried to learn. But she insisted that I recite word for word, with the repetition of the question that was in the book. If I had not learned my lesson she rebuked me. "And you think you are intelligent!" she would say witheringly. "What is the definition of grace, — actual grace and sanctifying grace? My fourth-grade pupils know more than you do."

I hadn't a doubt but that they did. I struggled on day by day, learning without question. I was in that agreeable and lethargic and almost bovine state of mind, filled with an animal content, not wishing to inquire into or question the dogmas I was learning. I made up my mind to accept what I did not understand, trusting light to come, as it sometimes did, in a blinding flash of exultation and realization. She criticized my housekeeping. "Here you

141

sit at your typewriter at ten o'clock and none of your dishes done yet. Supper and breakfast dishes besides.... And why don't you calcimine your ceiling? It's all dirty from woodsmoke."

She used to bring me vegetables from the garden of the Home, and I used to give her fish and clams. Once I gave her stamps and a dollar to send a present to a little niece and she was touchingly grateful. It made me suddenly realize that in spite of Charlie Schwab and his estate, the Sisters lived in complete poverty, owning nothing, holding all things in common.

She never came into the house directly but used to peer in the window or back door with a sepulchral whisper, "Is he here?" as though it were the devil himself she were inquiring after. And if Fred were there, he used to slam out of the other door to show his displeasure, greeting her through clenched teeth. I didn't blame him, nor did I blame her. She would probably have regarded any husband so, no matter how Catholic, how exemplary. She knew little of the world of men.

Finally the great day arrived and was a thing of the past. Teresa was baptized, she had become a member of the Mystical Body of Christ. I didn't know anything of the Mystical Body or I might have felt disturbed at being separated from her.

But I clutched her close to me and all that summer as I nursed her and bent over that tiny round face at my breast, I was filled with a deep happiness that nothing could spoil.

But the obstacles to my becoming a Catholic were there, shadows in the background of my life.

I had become convinced that I would become a Catholic, and yet I felt I was betraying the class to which I belonged, you my brother, the workers, the poor of the world, the class which Christ most loved and spent His life with. I wrote a few articles that summer for the *New Masses* but did no other work. My life was crowded because friends came and stayed with me, and some of them left their children. Two little boys, four and eight years old, joined the family for the summer and my days were full, caring for three children and cooking meals for from six to ten people three days a week.

Some few times I could get up to the village to Mass on Sunday, when I could leave the baby in trusted hands. But usually the gloom that descended on the household, the scarcely-voiced opposition, kept me from it. There were some feast days when I could slip off in the middle of the week and go to the little chapel on Charlie Schwab's grounds. There were "visits" I could make, unknown to others. I was committed, by the advice of a priest I consulted, to the plan of waiting, and trying to hold together the family. But I felt all along that when I took the irrevocable step it would mean that Teresa and I would be alone, and I did not want to be alone. I did not want to give up human love when it was dearest and tenderest.

During the month of August many of my friends, including my sister, went to Boston to picket in protest against the execution of Sacco and Vanzetti, which was drawing near. They were all arrested again and again.

Throughout the nation and the world, the papers featured the struggle for the lives of these two men. Radicals from all over the country gathered in Boston and articles describing those last days were published, poems were written. It was an epic struggle, a grand tragedy. One felt a sense of impending doom. These men were Catholics, inasmuch as they were Italians. Catholics by tradition, but they had rejected the Church.

While enjoying the fresh breeze, the feel of salt water against the flesh, the keen delight of living, the knowledge that these men were soon to pass from this physical earth, were soon to become dust, without consciousness, struck me like a physical blow. They were here now; in a few days they would be no more. They had become figures beloved by the workers. Their letters, the warm moving story of their lives, had been told. Everyone knew Dante, Sacco's young son. Everyone suffered with the young wife who clung with bitter passion to her husband. And Vanzetti with his large view, his sense of peace at his fate, was even closer to us all.

The day they died, the papers had headlines as large as those which proclaimed the outbreak of war. All the nation mourned. All the nation, that is, that is made up of the poor, the worker, the trade unionist, — those who felt most keenly the sense of solidarity, — that very sense of solidarity which made me gradually understand the doctrine of the Mystical Body of Christ whereby we are the members one of another.

Teresa's father was stricken over the tragedy. He had always been more an Anarchist than anything else in his philosophy. He did not eat for days. He sat around the house in a stupor of misery, sickened by the cruelty of life and of men. He had always taken refuge in nature as being more kindly, more beautiful and peaceful than the world of men. Now he could not even escape through nature, as he tried to escape so many problems in life.

During the time he was home he spent days and even nights out on the water fishing, so that for weeks I saw little of him. He stupefied himself in his passion for the water, sitting out on the bay in his boat. When he began to recover he submerged himself in maritime biology, collecting, reading only scientific books, and paying no attention to what went on around him. Only the baby interested him. She was his delight. Which made it, of course, the harder to contemplate the cruel blow I was going to strike him when I became a Catholic.

These pages are hard to write. The struggle was too personal. It was exceedingly difficult. The year passed and it was not until the following winter that the tension reached the breaking point. My health was bad, but a thorough examination at the Cornell clinic showed only nervous strain.

Finally with precipitation, with doubts on my part at my own unseemly haste, I made the resolution to bring an end to my hesitation and be baptized.

It was in December 1927, a most miserable day, and the trip was long from the city down to Tottenville, Staten Island. All the way on the ferry through the foggy bay I felt grimly that I was being too precipitate. I had no sense of peace, no joy, no conviction even that what I was doing was right. It was just something that I had to do, a task to be gotten through. I doubted myself when I allowed myself to think. I hated myself for being weak and vacillating. A most consuming restlessness was upon me so that I walked around and around the deck of the ferry, almost groaning in anguish of spirit. Perhaps the devil was on the boat.

Sister Aloysia was there waiting for me, to be my godmother. I do not know whether I had any other godparent. Father Hyland, gently, with reserve, with matter-of-factness, heard my confession and baptized me.

I was a Catholic at last though at that moment I never felt less the joy and peace and consolation which I know from my own later experiences religion can bring.

A year later my confirmation was indeed joyful and Pentecost never passes without a renewed sense of happiness and thanksgiving. It was only then that the feeling of uncertainty finally left me, never again to return, praise God!

Chapter Twelve

WHEAT AND COCKLE

Y OU ASK ME how I came to reject Communism. First of all, let this be understood, that I was a Communist in sympathy but with reservations scarcely formulated. I accepted Marxism as an economic theory and if I had been pinned down as to whether or not I was an atheist, I would probably have argued as you do: "How can we believe in a God who permitted such suffering and injustice in the world?"

Always at the bottom of my heart was the desire to believe, sometimes so faint as to be barely perceptible, at other times very strong. But I distrusted myself, my own emotional reactions and my own instability.

I did not believe in private property. I wanted to work for a state of society in which each should "work according to his ability and receive according to his need." That is Marx's definition of Communism. I did not believe that greedy and unjust men could be converted. I believed rather in the inevitability of revolution.

The three fundamentals of Communist belief are:

1. There is no other world than this; our last end is death and the grave, not God.

2. The ideal state is a Communist state in which there is no individual ownership but communal ownership.

3. Since there is no other way of achieving this except by violent means, then we must use those violent means. It is a cause worth dying for.

Of course this analysis is oversimplified, but it will serve to show how easy it is for idealistic young people, brought up without religion, to accept Communism. Paul Claudel says that youth demands the heroic. Someone else wrote once that he who is not a Socialist at the age of twenty has no heart, and he who is a Socialist at the age of thirty has no head.

I grieved at what I thought to be the necessity of subscribing to that first belief that our lives ended at the grave, but I thought it braver to accept it. I wholeheartedly subscribed to the other two fundamentals of Communism.

Now the creed to which I subscribe is like a battle cry, engraved on my heart — the *Credo* of the Holy Roman Catholic Church. Before, in those former times, I could say: "I shall sleep in the dust: and if thou seek me in the morning, I shall not be" (Job 7:21). Now I can say: "I know that my Redeemer liveth and in the last day I shall rise out of the earth. And I shall be clothed again with my skin, and in my flesh I shall see God. Whom I myself shall see and my eyes shall behold, and not another: this my hope is laid up in my bosom" (Job 19:25–27).

I had a conversation with John Spivak, the Communist writer, a few years ago and he said to me, "How can you believe? How can you believe in the Immaculate Conception, in the Virgin birth, in the Resurrection?" I could only say that I believe in the Roman Catholic Church and all She teaches. I have accepted Her authority with my whole heart. At the same time I want to point out to you that we are taught to pray for final perseverance. We are taught that faith is a gift and sometimes I wonder why some have it and some do not. I feel my own unworthiness and can never be grateful enough to God for His gift of faith. St. Paul tells us that if we do not correspond to the graces we receive, they will be withdrawn. So I believe also that we should walk in fear, "work out our salvation in fear and trembling."

As for those two other tenets to which the Communists subscribe, I still believe that our social order must be changed, that it is not right for property to be concentrated in the hands of the few. But I believe now with St. Thomas Aquinas that a certain amount of property is necessary for a man to lead a good life. I believe that we should work to restore the communal aspects of Christianity as well as some measure of private property for all.

I still believe that revolution is inevitable, leaving out Divine Providence. But with the help of God and by resorting to His sacraments and accepting the leadership of

Christ, I believe we can overcome revolution by a Christian revolution of our own, without the use of force.

I was part of the Communist movement in this country, inasmuch as I was a reporter, a writer. I was a member of the Socialist Party, later a member of the International Workers of the World, a member of many Communist affiliate organizations, but I was never a "signed up" member of the Communist Party.

It is true now as it was true from the beginning that no one was a signed member unless he attended the weekly meetings of his unit and conformed to the discipline of the Party which was and is rigorous. Usually writers (and it is true today of those working on the *New Masses, The Daily Worker,* and many other communist publications) are not members of the Party itself. One could be a member of an affiliate body and not a member of the political party. One could participate in the activities of the League for the Defense of Political Prisoners, the Anti-Imperialist League, for the Trade Union Unity League and many other organizations and still not be signed up as a member of the Party. There have always been so many affiliated and companion organizations started by the Party that it is hard to keep track of them all. Today one can give all his time to the work of the Scottsboro Defense Committee, the League for Peace and Democracy, the League for Spanish Democracy, and not be listed as a Communist Party member, but still be a Communist. These workers are quite distinct from

150

the "fellow-travelers" who are often liberals or Communist sympathizers, outside the movement yet helping it.

Today millions throughout the world consider themselves Communists even though their work, their family duties, prevent them from becoming party members. I played a very small part in the Communist movement in this country, but a writer can achieve a reputation in a movement and yet cannot say conscientiously that he does a great deal of work. That is, if he is honest. Because his name is signed to articles he may have a greater reputation than he deserves as a Communist.

Here is my attitude toward Communism now, after these many years. First of all, I consider it a heresy, a false doctrine but, as St. Augustine says, there is no false doctrine that does not contain certain elements of truth. I believe it is the failure of Christians which has brought about this heresy and that we will have to give an account for it.

My criticism of Christians in the past, and it *still* holds good of too many of them, is that they in fact deny God and reject Him. "Amen I say to you, as long as you did it to one of these my least brethren, you did it to me" (Matt. 25:40), Christ said, and today there are Christians who affront Christ in the Negro, in the poor Mexican, the Italian, yes and the Jew. Catholics believe that man is the temple of the Holy Ghost, that he is made to the image and likeness of God. We believe that of Jew and Gentile. We believe that all men are members or potential members of the Mystical Body of Christ and since there is no time with God, we must so consider each man whether he is atheist, Jew or Christian.

You ask do we really believe it, when we see our fellows herded like brutes in municipal lodging houses, tramping the streets and roads hungry, working at starvation wages or under an inhuman speed-up, living in filthy degrading conditions. Seeing many Christians denying Him, hating Him in the poor, is it any wonder a heresy has sprung up denying Him in word and deed?

The first commandment is that we should love the Lord our God. We can only show our love for God by our love for our fellows. "If any man say, I love God, and hateth his brother he is a liar. For he that loveth not his brother, whom he seeth, how can he love God, whom he seeth not?" (1 John 4:20).

For instance, there is the "scab," the strike-breaker, also a worker, and also of the poor and oppressed classes. Environment, slums, jails, bitter poverty, has played its part in developing viciousness and selfishness in him — granted. There are also good workers, honest men who have not been convinced of the justice of a strike, or of the fact that all arbitration has been used. Perhaps they are blind to the conditions of their fellows. They also are our brothers and can be educated, but not by clubs. There are the small farmers, ground down by corporations, perverted by our industrial system, weighed down with mortgage debts, who in turn oppress the transient worker. It is not only the transient worker who needs education, who needs our love and compassion.

There are also those soldiers blindly driven by their leaders into battle against a foe they do not know. Property-less, unemployed, just returned from one grueling war, sent out perhaps with the promise of land, of colonization, and finding themselves fighting again, their hatred aroused by hate-inspiring propaganda against the Communist. There may be not more than ten Communists in the regiment before them but they must kill all, the misleaders and those who are misled. Kill off the Communist to keep Communism down? I do not believe a heresy will be stopped in this way. Heresies also seem to thrive on persecution.

I will not deny that often the Communist more truly loves his brother, the poor and oppressed, than many so-called Christians. But, when in word and deed the Communist incites brother to kill brother, one class to hate and destroy other classes, then I cannot feel that his love is true. He is loving his friend, but not his enemy, who is also his brother. There is no brotherhood of man there, and there can be none without the Fatherhood of God.

Men are being tortured today in Soviet Russia. They are being jailed, their wives and children are being tortured, they are being put to death. Is this brotherly love? No, I grew not to believe in the brotherly love of the Communist. Human nature being what it is, I can only believe that men are capable of much goodness, through Christ who took upon Himself our human nature and exalted it.

Man lays claim to dignity through the fact that he is the temple of the Holy Spirit and made to the image and likeness of God. Take that from him and he is worse than a brute, because man has the power to think.

And yet what had attracted me first to Marxism was its recognition of the dignity of man and the dignity of his labor. But Christ Himself was a worker. St. Joseph, His foster father, was a worker. A man who works with his hands as well as with his head is an integrated personality. He is a co-creator, taking the raw materials God provided and creating food, clothing, and shelter and all manner of beautiful things.

But the Communist now exalts the proletariat, the property-less, and maintains in Russia a dictatorship of the proletariat at the expense of all other classes. And that dictatorship is maintained by the few, ruthlessly by violence.

Communism is a good word, a Christian word originally, but to expect to achieve a state of society in which all is held in common, where the state will "wither away" through state socialism, maintained through a dictatorship of the proletariat, this is impossible for a reasonable person to believe.

It is only through religion that communism can be achieved, and has been achieved over and over again.

Communists like to quote St. Peter's statement, "Servants, obey your masters." They forget his exhortation to work for a new heaven and a new earth, wherein justice dwelleth. Admitted that the servants are the oppressed, they cannot achieve justice without practicing justice themselves. They must first be right before they can insist on

154

right dealing from their masters. The servant is not greater than the master.

It was human love that helped me to understand divine love. Human love at its best, unselfish, glowing, illuminating our days, gives us a glimpse of the love of God for man. Love is the best thing we can know in this life, but it must be sustained by an effort of the will. It is not just an emotion, a warm feeling of gratification. It must lie still and quiet, dull and smoldering, for periods. It grows through suffering and patience and compassion. We must suffer for those we love, we must endure their trials and their sufferings, we must even take upon ourselves the penalties due their sins. Thus we learn to understand the love of God for His creatures. Thus we understand the Crucifixion.

It is hard to explain. It is difficult to make myself clear. If St. Paul, to whom Christ Himself spoke, saw things as through a glass, darkly, how can I hope to make things clear to you? I have only tried to put down what I do understand, urging you again not to discredit Christianity because of the faults of Christians.

Perhaps you will not see my point at all as you read this, but I pray that you too will be led by the Holy Ghost from darkness into light. Even the little I see is light to me in the darkest of days and hours. And I could not breathe or live without that light which I have now — the light of Faith which has been given to me by a merciful God Who is the Light of the world.

Chapter Thirteen

YOUR THREE
OBJECTIONS

Y OU SAY THAT religion is morbid. This is quite a natural feeling on your part and it is a very common
attitude of Communists toward religion. If those who
spend several hours a day in prayer, and hours more in
spiritual reading, as St. Teresa did, in a willful search for
God, had these feelings, these struggles — how much more
those who are scarcely touched by faith or hope?

You know the reaction of my friends to religion, that it
is a deliberate turning away from life. We Catholics know,
with a supernatural knowledge, not with a worldly knowledge, that this is not so, just as we know the existence of
God and love Him with our will, which is a power of
our souls.

St. Teresa struggled for twenty years, she said, to avoid
the occasions of sin. To know what she was talking about,
what she meant by sin, it is necessary to understand the
situation she was in. She had entered the convent at the
age of eighteen. The Carmelite convent was a large one,
containing so many nuns that it was difficult to feed them

all. It was the custom of the day to send unmarried daughters, widows, ladies who wished to retire from the world to the convent, and yet they did not retire from the world. There were a great many visitors. St. Teresa herself said that one of the reasons so many visitors came was to bring food to the nuns, and they received their callers because there was so little food in the convent that they needed to eke out their resources in that way. Later when St. Teresa was making her foundations of the reformed Carmelites, she saw to it that her nuns had enough to eat.

St. Teresa knew that she was far from leading the life she wished to lead when she entered the convent. She wished to give herself up wholly to God. She wished everything she did, every word she said, to tend to that end. But she was a joyful creature. The story is that she went to be received in the convent in a bright red dress. She was full of vitality, life. She wished to live abundantly. The very qualities in her which urged her to give herself to God, drew her to her fellows. She had an abundant love for them, an interest in them, and there was much time spent in conversations.

The more her life was involved with her friends, the more she was drawn to them, the more she felt she was drawing away from God. She was making little account of venial sins, she said; she was not avoiding the occasions of them. She felt that she was a sinful creature and said so many times in her autobiography. This does not mean anything scandalous — that the convent ladies sat around and received unseemly visits, ate or drank to excess, or indulged in vicious talk or gossip.

But St. Teresa had so great a desire for perfection that any time engaged in idle talk (the most innocent idle talk) seemed to her to be deliberately stolen from God. She knew what she wanted, she knew that there was a better life for her, but she had to struggle to attain it.

She tells how she was kept from prayer. "The sadness I felt on entering the oratory was so great that it required all the courage I had to force myself in. They say of me that my courage is not slight, and it is known that God has given me a courage beyond that of a woman; but I have made a bad use of it."

She told, too, of watching the hour glass, of how she was filled with distractions, of what a constant hard struggle it was to force herself to prayer and spiritual reading. And these struggles went on for twenty years!

"I wished to live," she wrote, "but I saw clearly that I was not living, but rather wrestling with the shadow of death; there was no one to give me life, and I was not able to take it."

This is the "morbidness" that you mean, I know. If St. Teresa, with her knowledge and insight and the graces God gave her to go on struggling, felt that she was wrestling with the shadow of death, how one who knows nothing of religion must shy off from it every time the matter enters his consciousness!

The shadow of death that she spoke of was the life she was leading, purposeless, disordered, a constant succumbing to second-best, to the less-than-perfect which she desired. But human nature will try to persuade us that the life of prayer is death, is a turning away from life.

As a convert I can say these things, knowing how many times I turned away, almost in disgust, from the idea of God and giving myself up to Him. I know the feeling of uneasiness, of weariness, the feeling of strain put upon the soul from driving it, instead of abandoning it to God. But I do not know how anyone can persist in the search for God without the assistance of the Church and the advice of those confessors with the experience of generations behind them.

The thing you do not understand is the elemental fact that our beginning and our last end is God. Once that fact is accepted, half the struggle is won. If we wish to go on struggling, not to be content with the minimum of virtue, of duty done, of "just getting by," then we should account it a great honor that God has given us these desires, to serve Him and to use ourselves completely in His service.

You do not see this, you do not believe it. Every now and then, when you think of religion in your busy life, you end by turning from it with aversion. You are young, and you have not yet really felt the need, the yearning toward God. You have not been in such agony and misery that you turned to One whom you knew not and said, "God help me!" Or if you did, you were ashamed of doing it afterward, feeling it to be cowardice to turn in misery to a God in Whom you did not believe.

I felt this despair when I lay there in jail for fifteen days, contemplating the fundamental misery of human existence, a misery which would remain even if social justice were achieved and a state of Utopia prevailed. For you cannot pace the floor of a barred cell, or lie on your back on a hard cot watching a gleam of sunlight travel slowly, oh, so slowly, across the room, without coming to the realization that until the heart and soul of man is changed, there is no hope of happiness for him.

On the other hand, you have not felt the ecstasy, the thankfulness, the joy, which caused the Psalmist to cry out, "My heart and my flesh rejoice for the living God." "My soul longeth and fainteth for the courts of the Lord" (Ps. 83:1).

St. John of the Cross, who lived at the same time as St. Teresa and was her good friend, tells about the different stages of prayer and how the first state is the purgative state. He explains how though we feel this joy and this longing of God, a joy which is so sweet that even the remembrance of it is a constant spur to us, still our own imperfections give us constant suffering and unease, and the struggle for the spiritual life is a wearisome one, and that we must not expect to find ease in prayer. He makes us understand this distaste, this recoil from religion. This lethargy comes from a consciousness of the imminence of the struggle, the fact that it is unceasing and will go on to death, and we often think that sheer thoughtless paganism would be a relief.

No one but God knows how long I struggled, how I turned to Him, and turned from Him, again and again. I, too, felt that distaste. I, too, felt that religion had a morbid quality. It is the struggle of the flesh against the spirit. It is the struggle of the natural man against that in him that is divine. (I am going to write you later about the flesh and the spirit, the sensual and the spiritual, for you have an entirely wrong idea as to what Karl Adam calls "the antitheses with which Christianity is concerned.")

I can understand what you mean by morbid, and can understand how no matter how often you are drawn you are also repelled. If you only knew, and could in intellectual humility submit yourself to the rule which makes all so plain and clear!

We have "a rule of life" that is easy to follow, provided we listen to the wise counsel of such people as St. Teresa, St. Francis de Sales, de Caussade, Father Considine. I mention these names because they are the first ones that come to mind.

St. Teresa understood that weariness of the soul. St. Francis tells us to be gentle with ourselves. De Caussade tells us to abandon ourselves to Divine Providence, and Father Considine tells us to have more faith in God as a kind Father Who is so far above our earthly fathers that He will forgive us all our sins, even the greatest, Who will not give us a stone when we ask for bread.

We are taught that our souls need exercise just as our body does, otherwise it will never be healthy and well, and if the soul is not in a healthy state, of course we feel morbid. Prayer is the exercise for the soul, just as bending and stretching is the exercise of the body. It is intellectual pride, the arrogance of youth, which makes the physical act of prayer difficult.

You submit yourself to the dogma of Communism, you accept the authority of Karl Marx and Lenin, you accept the philosophy of Communism and know while you accept it that you are accepting a "hard saying," that in all likelihood you will be persecuted for this acceptance. Perhaps the main trouble is that to you Christianity is too simple. To you Christianity is the accepted thing, so you rebel, and knowing that your rebellion deprives your soul of life, you turn on religion and call it morbid.

◆ ◆ ◆

It has been only with a great deal of hesitation that I take up the second objection you have to religion. (It is interesting to note that your objections, as the objections of most Communists and agnostics, are to the *Catholic* Faith. The words *Catholic* and *religion* go together in your mind.)

Blasphemies one hesitates to set down on paper, they are so horrifying. Many would put your second objection in this category. One nun to whom I mentioned it shuddered involuntarily, but she did not try to meet it. And in the past when I have heard it, and all Catholics have heard it many times, I, too, did not try to answer. You made your objection in good faith, not in any spirit of hatred or malice, and I have heard it made in good faith before. So I think it is just as well to try to meet it though it is hard, well-nigh impossible, to talk of such things to one who has no faith. I am somewhat heartened by something I read this morning in Faber, "It is our duty as well as our privilege to look into this mystery."

You say you object to religion because it has a cannibalistic aspect which revolts you. A twelve-year-old girl who was reared with no knowledge of the Christian religion said almost the same thing to me last winter. "Catholics believe that they eat the Body and Blood of Christ, don't they?" she said, with a look of distaste. She, too, did not mean to blaspheme. She was honest.

I suppose I never felt this objection, this repulsion, because long before I became a radical I had felt deeply the mysteries of faith, not *the* Faith, but faith nevertheless. Remember, I read the Bible when I was twelve, and I knew what my conscience was, and what was good and evil. I had accepted the doctrine of the Holy Eucharist. So when I came back to God there was not that difficulty to overcome.

It is easy for a little child to accept unquestioningly. That is why the League of the Militant Godless is so anxious to keep religion from little children. Because they know they will accept it, and though they fall away afterward perhaps, in an arrogant and adventurous adolescence, still it is not so insuperably difficult to come back to it because there is some kernel of truth lying hidden there in the soul. You never had any religious instruction when you were a child, so the difficulty is there for you.

If you know the New Testament at all (and you ought to look into it if you do not know it, for many Communists express an admiration for the Man Jesus, and I.W.W.'s in the old days used to speak of "Comrade Jesus"), you will find there that the first to whom Christ taught this doctrine of the Blessed Sacrament turned from Him. This teaching, that Christ would be their daily bread, was so simple, so elemental a thing, in spite of its mystery, that children and the simplest and least of people in the world could accept it.

St. Teresa says that Christ is disguised as bread so that we will not fear to approach Him — so that we can go to Him in confidence, daily, needing Him daily as we need our physical bread.

We are not, most of us, capable of exalted emotion, save rarely. We are not capable always of feelings of love, awe, gratitude, and repentance. So Christ has taken the form of bread that we may more readily approach Him, and feeding daily, assimilating Christ so that it is not we but Christ working in us, we may be made more capable of understanding and realizing and loving Him.

Yes, in bread Christ has become so simple — has condescended so far, that a child can eat the Sacred Food with love and gratitude. He said that we would be scandalized, so it is no use for me to be surprised and horrified at the bluntness of your objection. Even the nearest and dearest of His friends dispersed and fled, not realizing the mystery of the Redemption, that Christ was laying down His life for all men.

When He prayed in agony in the garden — when the weight of our sins descended upon Him, all the sins that had been and that would be committed throughout the world forever after; when He suffered all the temptations, all the horror, all the remorse for the rest of the world — His disciples did not understand that either. He watched and suffered alone in His agony. He had told them that the next day He was to die. And in spite of His miracles they paid so little attention to His words that they slept, as the Friend they loved most in the world struggled against the thought of His death. They left Him alone, they slept, and the next day they fled, so little did they understand His teachings, though they had been with Him for three years. They did not understand even after they had eaten with Him at the Last Supper. They did not understand until the Holy Spirit descended upon them and it was *given* to them to understand.

So how can I understand or try to tell you about it? If they who lived with Him, who could see Him as man, eat with Him, sleep with Him, and wander with Him through the countryside, if they were "offended" and dispersed, how can I try to tell you what is in my heart? I do not ask myself, "How can I try to overcome your objection?" Only

God can do that. I am not trying to convert you, but just trying not to let go unchallenged your objections, for fear that my not answering would seem to you a kind of denial of Him Whom I love.

There is the question, why did Christ institute this Sacrament of His Body and Blood? And the answer is very simple. It was because He loved us and wished to be with us. "My delights are to be with the children of men." He made us and He loves us. His presence in the Blessed Sacrament is the great proof of that love.

St. Teresa of Avila said that we should meditate more on the love of God for us, rather than our love for Him. And she emphasizes His sacred Humanity and says that by never losing sight of that it is easier for us to realize that love. She is always talking about the Man Jesus.

But it is hard to understand the love of God for us. We pray daily to increase in the love of God because we know that if we love a person very much, all things become easy to us and delightful. We want, rather unreasonably, sensible feelings of love. St. Teresa says that the only way we can measure the love we have for God, is the love we have for our fellows. So by working for our fellows we come to love them. That you understand, for you believe that you are working for them when you give hours every morning to the distribution of literature, climbing tenement-house stairs, knocking at doors, suffering rebuffs, enduring heat and cold, weariness and hardships to bring to them what you consider a gospel which will set them free.

And if you and I love our faulty fellow-human beings, how much more must God love us all? If we as human parents, can forgive our children any neglect, any crime, and work and pray patiently to make them better, how much more does God love us?

You may say perhaps: "How do we know He does, if there is a He!" And I can only answer that we know it because He is here present with us today in the Blessed Sacrament on the altar, that He never has left us, and that by daily going to Him for the gift of Himself as daily bread, I am convinced of that love. I have the Faith that feeding at that table has nourished my soul so that there is life in it, and a lively realization that there is such a thing as the love of Christ for us.

It took me a long time as a convert to realize the presence of Christ as Man in the Sacrament. He is the same Jesus Who walked on earth, Who slept in the boat as the tempest arose, Who hungered in the desert, Who prayed in the garden, Who conversed with the woman by the well, Who rested at the house of Martha and Mary, Who wandered through the cornfields, picking the ears of corn to eat.

Jesus is there as Man. He is there, Flesh and Blood, Soul and Divinity. He is our leader Who is always with us. Do you wonder that Catholics are exultant in this knowledge, that their Leader is with them? "I am with you all days, even to the consummation of the world."

Christ is bread on our altars because bread is the staple of the world, the simplest thing in the world, something of which we eat and never get tired. We will always have bread whether it is corn, wheat, or rye, or whatever it is made from. We will always find wherever we go some staple which is called bread.

We eat to sustain life. It is the most elemental thing we do. For the life of the body we need food. For the life of the soul we need food. So the simplest, most loving, most thorough thing Christ could do before He died, was to institute the Blessed Sacrament. He did this by taking a piece of bread which He blessed and broke and gave to his disciples saying, "Take ye and eat. This is My Body." And taking the chalice He gave thanks, and gave to them saying: "Drink ye all of this for This is My Blood." And He told them to do this in commemoration of Him.

If you sat and thought forever and ever, you could not think of any way for Christ to remain with us which would bring us closer to Him. I could keep on writing and writing and never come to the end of this, but I won't. I only hope that in your sincerity, which acknowledges my sincerity, you will read me through. You know how much emphasis Christ put on the "little ones" who are the majority. Not only the children, but the poor and helpless. Those without learning, when it comes to reading books about the Blessed Sacrament or dialectic materialism, are another instance of what I mean.

With all my writing to you the products of my thought on this subject, I can only end with the words of Jesus,

"I thank Thee, O Father, Lord of heaven and earth, that thou hast hid these things from the wise and prudent, and hast revealed them unto babes: Even so, Father. For so it seemed good in thy sight."

For so it seemed good in His sight!

♦ ♦ ♦

Your third objection is that you could not understand the problem of evil. Who am I to try to answer that great and grave objection that has been made so many times in the face of tragedy? But St. Peter said that we must strive to give a reason for the faith that is in us.

During the last winter I have thought a great deal about this, knowing that I should some day sit down and write it to you. Again and again the problem of evil has come forward, has been discussed; but it is hard to state the problem and try to give logically the conclusions reached by one simple person. According to the *Catholic Encyclopedia,* "Evil in a large sense, may be described as the sum of the opposition which experience shows to exist in the universe, to the desires and needs of individuals."

Leaving out "moral evil" which I am sure you recognize since you never deliberately say to yourself, "This is wrong; I am going to do it," and since you recognize your duty to your neighbor; leaving out metaphysical evil, since we will not here deal with earthquakes, cyclones, floods, and the predatory instincts of animals, — there remains "physical" evil, which is the "evil" to which you refer.

"Physical evil," the *Encyclopedia* continues, "includes all that causes harm to man, whether by bodily injury, by thwarting his natural desires, or by preventing the full development of his powers, either in the order of nature directly, or through the various social conditions under which mankind naturally exists. Physical evils due to nature are sickness, accident, death. Poverty, oppression, and some forms of disease are instances of evil arising from imperfect social organization. Mental suffering, such as anxiety, disappointment, and remorse, and the limitation of intelligence which prevents human beings from attaining to the full comprehension of their environment, are congenital forms of evil which vary in character and degree according to natural disposition and social circumstances."

So, you say, if God created everything, He created evil — God is responsible for it, and you don't like that kind of a God, and, not liking Him, refuse to believe in Him.

I will agree with you that we believe God created everything and that He is all Good. But we believe too that evil is a negative thing, not a positive thing. That is an absence of Good.

We also believe that God granted free will to man, and how great and terrible a gift that is! How incomparably better it is of our own free will, — of our own choice, that we should choose the Good. How much better is that love which we give freely, as free men and not as slaves. How great is that liberty which the Church teaches us we have.

170

We admit that our free will is often limited by circumstances, and priests show that they recognize this when they deal with the question of mortal sin, which is only mortal sin when committed with full consent of the will.

Fear, insecurity, hunger, anger, love, — all these things go to influence the will.

Do you remember the man in *The Black Pit,* that Communist play which was at the Civic Repertory Theatre some time ago? The youth did not wish to become a company spy, but he was influenced by circumstances — his poverty, the approaching confinement of his wife, his brother's crippled state, his previous sentence in jail, — to commit what he knew to be a mortal sin, and injury to his comrades. But even though his will was limited, the audience felt that he was weak, that he should have been strong and that he should have sacrificed everything, wife, child, and family and even his own liberty, rather than his integrity as a worker.

Another thing about free will. Do you remember our friend, Lilian, whose eighteen-year-old son turned on the gas and committed suicide some years ago? She stayed with me, you remember, for some months after the tragedy, and I, too, was bowed to the earth with it. And one day she said to me, in the midst of her grief, accepting the tragic act of her son, "He had to do it. It was his own will. I always let the boys choose the way they should go. I did not wish him to consider me and to stick to me from a sense of duty. I loved his adventurousness and his freedom and when he came and stayed with me I knew it was because he wanted to. I would not have him back. If he wanted to go, it was up to him."

It may seem strange and even sacrilegious, but from this woman with her distorted sense of values — she had no faith of any kind — I learned much. I remember it came to me with a sense of shock, — my first realization of how great and terrible a gift is free will, and how it ennobles man.

Perhaps many people would say that they would rather be without it. Perhaps they say, "Why did God allow me to do this, to commit these sins, to store up for myself this punishment?" But how can any reasonable human being deny that the gift of free will is a great and ennobling gift?

You remember, then, the story of Adam and Eve and the garden. They chose to defy God, to set their wills against His, and since then "all nature travaileth and groaneth." Since that time there is sin and suffering in the world, and a constant battle to fight. Heaven must be taken by violence. That is the great war which has been going on always, and when I think of Communism, how small and petty and futile class war seems! For those who wish the struggle, the heroic, let them engage themselves in taking heaven by violence.

I have treated the question so sparingly. I have only suggested things to you, brought to your attention my own rambling thoughts on the question, which above all questions has perplexed the greatest minds. Mind you, I am

not thinking that I am solving any problem. I am just trying to give you my own reactions to the questions that
bother you.

I confess that what I do not understand I let pass by.
There are some problems that I like to grapple with, and
think about, but I do not force myself. I am not disturbed by problems, and I further confess (and you will
not despise me because I am a woman and women are like
that) that I avoid thinking, very often, of things I do not
understand.

It is so much easier to abandon oneself to Divine Providence and think of those comforting words, "Blessed are
those who have not seen and yet have believed." And we
certainly are blessed, I assure you, and I thank God for so
blessing me.

Gratitude brought me into the Church and that gratitude grows, and the first word my heart will utter, when
I face my God is "Thanks." And that goes, with the help
of God, for the gift of free will even though it entails sin,
evil, suffering and death.

You remember that terrible scene in *Point Counter Point*
by Aldous Huxley where the child dies in long-drawn-out
agony? I thought then as I read that here was a man who
was being harrowed by contemplating the physical suffering of the world and was almost hating God for it in his
rebellion against it. Strangely enough I did not mind his
hating God so much as I humanly minded the suffering of

that child. A Jewish convert said to me once, "The Communists hate God, and the Catholics love Him. But they are both facing Him, directing their attention to Him. They are not indifferent. Communists are not in so bad a case as those who are indifferent. It is the lukewarm that He will spew out of His mouth."

So I would rather that you, too, would think of the suffering of a child and hate God than be indifferent to Him. Then I could talk to you and you would listen.

Do you remember Ivan, in Dostoevsky's *Brothers Kara-mazov* and his rebellion against free will? "Why should man know that diabolical good and evil when it costs so much? The whole world of knowledge is not worth that child's prayer to 'dear kind God'! I say nothing of the sufferings of grown-up people, they have eaten the apple, damn them, and the devil take them all! But these little ones!"

But leaving the problem of the child for a moment, think of love and of suffering for yourself. All you know is human love. But St. Teresa said that we can measure our love for God by our love for our fellow human beings. For a long time I thought she meant it just as a general statement of love for our fellows. But it came to me later that she was thinking of the love of a woman for a man, a man for a woman — human love.

When you love, you are absorbed by the thought of the one you love. It is there always in the background of your thoughts. You live more intensely, you feel more vividly. The sunshine is brighter; beauty and pain are intensified.

And if you love God really and vitally, you will think not that this is a temptation of the flesh but that this love which has descended upon you can be used as a rule by which you can measure and increase your love for God.

You are conscious always of the presence in this world with you of another human being who is bound to you in some strange way, by some spell, so that you are obsessed by the thought of him. But what about God? I wonder am I continually conscious, in the background of my thoughts, of His presence in my life? Am I practicing the presence of God, as the phrase is? Because of God is each task ennobled, each contact vivified, each moment more intense? Is the love of Christ, in other words, driving me on?

When one is in love, one cannot conceive of not being in love. Life seems dull and drab to contemplate without this vital emotion. Can one conceive of life without God, separated from Him? Yes, human love is a good comparison, a good measuring rod. And you will agree with me that the desire for sacrifice comes with love. What do you suppose was the emotion that upheld Sacco and Vanzetti when they were imprisoned for those eight long years? You have read their letters, and you know as I do, that it was the love of their fellows, a desire to suffer and sacrifice themselves for them. If the love of man can lead one to such an exalted state — what of the love of God? Think of the numbers of men who have died for the love of God, holding out their arms to share in Christ's sufferings.

Yes, love, great love — and who wishes to be mediocre in love? — brings with it a desire for suffering. The love of God can become so overwhelming that it wishes to do everything for the Beloved, to endure hunger, cold, sleeplessness in an ecstasy of zeal and enthusiasm. There is a love so great that the Beloved is all and oneself nothing, and this realization, leading to humility, a real joyful humility which desires to do the least, the meanest, the hardest as well as the most revolting tasks, to crush the pride of self, to abandon oneself fully, to abandon even the desire for heroism. To prostrate oneself upon the earth, that noble earth, that beloved soil which Christ made sacred and significant for us by His Blood with which He watered it.

You may say, yes, admitted the desire to suffer every pain and anguish for oneself, but what of the sufferings of others? And you may say to me — could you stand by and see your child strung screaming by the thumbs in some Mexican jail — they have done that even to children in Mexico — without being so convulsed by hate, if not for God, for those fiendish creatures who perpetrate the torture? Could you love them as you are bidden to do? Could you see your ten-year-old child convulsed and screaming in an agony from some disease and not question the goodness of the God that permits such things?

And I can only say to you in answer — and I weep with misery and anguish as I write it — that even so, I am begging God to reinforce my fortitude so that if such horrors should come upon me (and thank God we cannot foresee such things), and all my human nature were convulsed even to madness, my will — my free will which God has given me — would hold me rigidly in His presence so that in life, which contains such unbearable and terrible things, as well as in death, I will choose Him and hold fast to Him. *For Who else is there?* Would you have me choose Nothingness?

Yes, I tell you, it has been hard to write all this. It has taken me more than a year to do it. All of it is addressed to you with love and with yearning and because there are many of you, and because God has given me writing to do as a vocation, I write.

And I beg you to read and to believe me when I say that I believe that neither life nor death, nor things past nor things to come, can separate me from love of God, provided that by using that gift of free will, I direct my choice toward Him.

For Further Reading on Dorothy Day

Dorothy Day
Selected Writings
Edited and with an Introduction
by Robert Ellsberg
ISBN 1-57075-581-7

Christopher Award Winner

"To read this collection of the published work of Dorothy Day
is to be drawn back into the world of faith and work that
defined her life and the Catholic Worker movement she created."
—*The New York Times*

Dorothy Day
Portraits by Those Who Knew Her
Rosalie G. Riegle
ISBN 1-57075-664-3

Now in paperback, with over forty photographs

"As long as this book survives, there is little danger that the memory
of Dorothy Day will pruned of all that made her fully human."
—*Sojourners*

"A highly inspirational book for those who love peace, joy,
and putting Christ's words into practice."
—*St. Anthony Messenger*